Expedition to Disaster

Expedition to Disaster

Philip Matyszak

Pen & Sword
MILITARY

First published in Great Britain in 2012 by
Pen & Sword Military
an imprint of
Pen & Sword Books Ltd
47 Church Street
Barnsley
South Yorkshire
S70 2AS

ISBN 978-1-84884-887-0

Typeset in 11pt Ehrhardt by
Mac Style, Beverley, E. Yorkshire

Printed and bound in the UK by CPI Group (UK) Ltd, Croydon, CRO 4YY

Pen & Sword Books Ltd incorporates the Imprints of Pen & Sword
Aviation, Pen & Sword Family History, Pen & Sword Maritime, Pen &
Sword Military, Pen & Sword Discovery, Wharncliffe Local History,
Wharncliffe True Crime, Wharncliffe Transport, Pen & Sword Select,
Pen & Sword Military Classics, Leo Cooper, The Praetorian Press,
Remember When, Seaforth Publishing and Frontline Publishing.

For a complete list of Pen & Sword titles please contact
PEN & SWORD BOOKS LIMITED
47 Church Street, Barnsley, South Yorkshire, S70 2AS, England
E-mail: enquiries@pen-and-sword.co.uk
Website: www.pen-and-sword.co.uk

Contents

List of Plates

1. View of Athenian tombs near the Keremaikos. Here Greeks who fell in battle were buried in an annual ceremony. Every effort was made to retrieve corpses from a battlefield and bring them home to Athens. (Photograph courtesy of Jeremy Day)
2. Temple at Egesta on Sicily. This construction is contemporary with the Athenian expedition, and indeed it may be that the elements of the temple which are incomplete are so because building work was overtaken by the events described in this book. (Photograph courtesy of Jeremy Day)
3. Modern view of the Syracuse harbour from Epipolae via the Euryalus Pass, with Plemmyrium at the top right of the picture. (Photograph courtesy of Dr Nigel Pollard)
4. The remains of the Temple of Apollo in Syracuse. Enough of the building has survived to show the early Doric design, with possible Ionic influences. (Photograph courtesy of Dr Nigel Pollard)
5. Part of the peripteros of the temple of Athena on Ortygia in Syracuse, now incorporated into the body of the Duomo (cathedral). (Photograph courtesy of Dr Nigel Pollard)
6. The quarries at Syracuse where the Athenian prisoners ended their days. (Photograph courtesy of Jeff Champion)
7. A fragment of stone relief from the Parthenon, the best contemporary evidence of how rowers sat in a trireme. (Photograph Philip Matyszak)
8. The *Olympias* under way – this is very probably how triremes looked while making long ocean crossings. The mixture of people sitting and standing on the upper decks had to be carefully arranged to keep the ship stable. (Photograph courtesy of The Trireme Trust)
9. The head-on ram shows the area of the bows where the Syracusans reinforced the cat's heads (top either side of ram) to make their ships less seaworthy but better than the Athenians in a close-quarter head-to-head. Note that usually a ship rigged for action had the sail removed. (Photograph courtesy of The Trireme Trust)

List of Maps

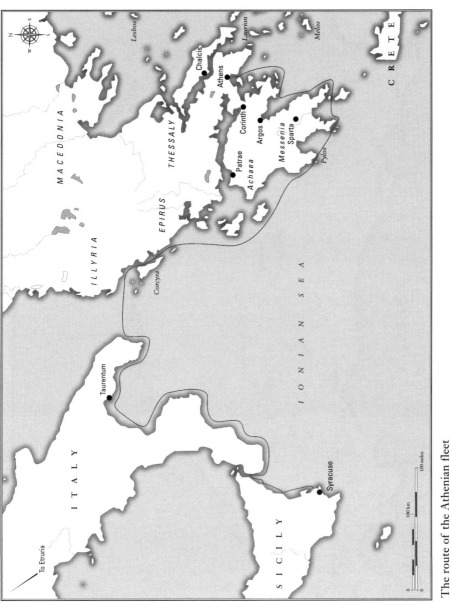

The route of the Athenian fleet

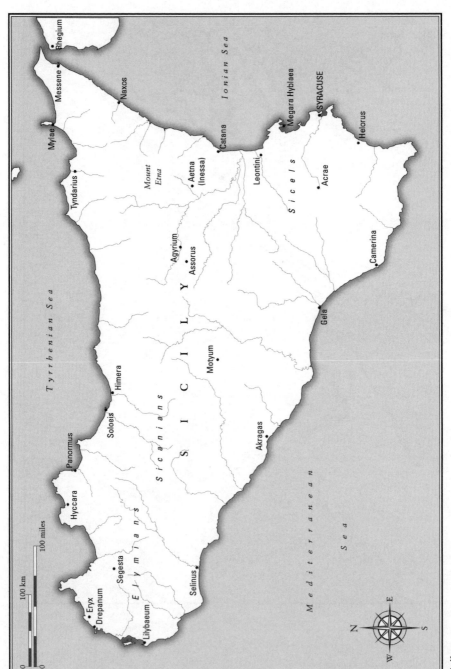

Sicily.

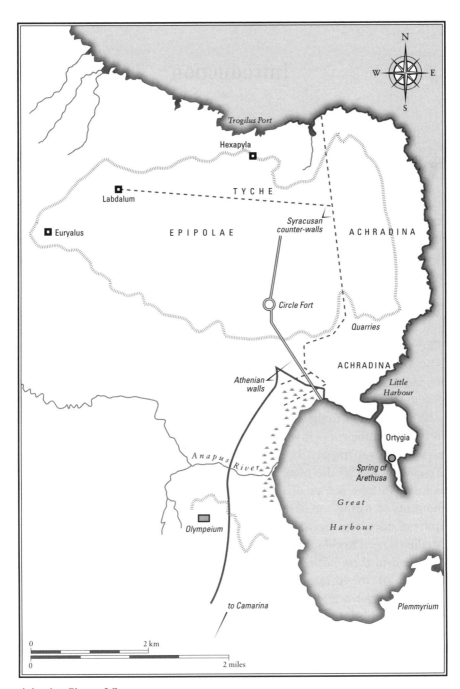

Athenian Siege of Syracuse.

Introduction

Why tell the story of the Athenian expedition to Sicily and the disastrous aftermath? There are a number of reasons. The first is that this story has not received the attention it deserves from historians. Even today, over 2,000 years since the last Athenian hoplite fought and died under the walls of Syracuse, perhaps the best version of the story is that of the historian Thucydides, who undoubtedly talked face to face with some who took part in that ill-fated mission.

However, the world has moved on. Many things that were so obvious to Thucydides and his contemporaries that they needed no explanation are only now being re-discovered through painstaking excavation and reconstruction. The challenge in telling this story was to supplement the story of Thucydides with explanations and detail that make it accessible to the modern reader while losing none of the drama and urgency of the original narrative.

Which takes us to the second reason for writing this book – a reason that in itself is sufficient – it is a rattling good tale. The story of the Athenian expedition is a tragedy, as powerful and moving as any by Sophocles or Aeschylus, and all the more so because this is a story of real people and events. We have scenes of pathos, drama and high adventure. There are moments of daring and despair. And through it all shines that irrepressible spirit of adventure by which the Greeks of the fifth century powered the Mediterranean world into a new and better era. There are battles on sea and land, and in these not only are we inspired by the old-fashioned Homeric heroism of the protagonists, but we also admire the ingenuity and occasionally downright sneakiness of the stratagems.

There is much to be learned from this story. The ability of both sides in the struggle to innovate on the fly, adapting their tactics as the situation changes, should be an example to any military or business leader. This narrative is also a cautionary tale of the dangers of complacency, and of how commanders who fail to show initiative and leadership can drag an enterprise to disaster almost as fast as inspirational, charismatic but misguided leaders can do. The Athenian expedition was cursed with both types of leader as well as with competent journeyman generals who, in the style of the best tragic heroes, could clearly see impending disaster that the stubbornness of their commanders left them powerless to avert.

We know and rightly admire much about the Athenians. And in this story too they show much that is admirable. The soaring ambition that lay behind the expedition, the eagerness with which challenges were met and overcome … these things command admiration. We can applaud the audacity of the entire adventure and the skill with which the Athenian commanders initially ran rings around the leaden-footed Syracusan defence. But none of this admiration should blind us to the fact that in this drama the Athenians are the villains.

When the purpose of an adroit political manoeuvre is to turn an unsuspecting ally into a conquered subject, our admiration for the adroitness must be matched by distaste for the purposes for which it is used. The speeches quoted here are marvels of persuasion (even more powerful in the original Greek), yet all too often the purpose of such persuasion is to gull listeners into voluntarily giving up hard-won freedoms.

The brilliance of the Periclean era had its dark side. Athens was a democracy, but it was also a state that had many more slaves than voters. Many of these slaves worked and died in abominable conditions in the silver mines at Laurion, the very mines that paid for the marble stoas on which the philosophers expounded their intellectual breakthroughs. Both the Sicilian expedition and previous excursions were in part massive slave raids in which the Athenians sought new victims to work their silver mines in Attica and Thrace. Likewise, though the Parthenon on the Athenian acropolis is an architectural triumph, its soaring beauty would be more of a testimonial to the human spirit if the money to build it had not been extorted and embezzled from reluctant subjects who had, until a few years previously, thought they were friends and allies.

It would be unjust and hypocritical to judge the Athenians by the standards of modern morality, and this book does not do so. If this were the case, the verdict would be yet more damning. All these criticisms, and more, were levelled at the Athenians by contemporary Greeks, who took as dim a view as any modern left-leaning academic of the shameless and expansionist imperialism of fifth-century Athens.

There are other echoes from the past that still resonate today. Expressions such as 'We are an empire, and empires create their own reality' could have come straight from the mouth of any Athenian demagogue, but these particular words reflect the ill-judged hubris of a member of the recent Bush administration in the USA. Likewise, in the year of a presidential election, American voters might like to consider how the silver-tongued Alcibiades charmed the Athenians into their ill-advised and ultimately disastrous venture.

Where similarities are to be found, they come with hindsight: where the voters are railroaded into war by a mixture of dissimulation and fear-mongering, and where that war is itself poorly planned and executed by squabbling commanders who have – literally, in the case of the Athenians – given insufficient thought to their exit strategy.

Nevertheless, while perhaps this introduction and the conclusion are places where one might moralize on the lessons of the story, the reader is left to draw his or her own conclusions from the text itself. But be aware that the ultimate source of this story, the historian Thucydides, has slanted his tale and we should read it as the author intended – as a morality story, not for today, nor of that time, but for the ages. And we should read it less for the lessons it teaches us for today than because it is an epic narrative well worth reading for its own sake.

As ever, the name on the front cover of a book does an injustice to the many people who made willing and substantial contributions to the project. I owe thanks to Nigel Pollard, who shared both his knowledge and pictures of Syracuse, to the Trireme Trust, whose splendid pictures illustrate the text as much as the expertise of its members have informed my discussions of trireme warfare. Without their insights this would have been an inferior text. Where I have blundered, the error lies in my inability to understand rather than theirs to explain.

Again I have to thank both Cambridge University in England and the University of British Columbia in Vancouver for their generous support of my research and the access they have given to essential journals and texts. Further thanks are due to the community of historians, especially Adrian Goldsworthy, with whom I have discussed ideas and re-fought battles.

Finally, to my wife, Malgosia who dragged an obsessive away from the keyboard for things like meals, only to put up with trireme battles enthusiastically re-created with bread rolls as I worked out the current state of play in Syracuse harbour. For all the social occasions missed, family members ignored and for a cat that would otherwise have starved to death – I owe you.

Chapter 1

Events Leading to a Very Warm Cold War

Gentlemen, you have an empire. No one in your situation can afford to consider what is right and what is wrong … if you won't focus on your own best interests you might as well chuck it all in and take up philanthropy.

The Athenian leader Cleon advocates
massacring the population of Mytilene[1]

In the year 416 BC, the Athenians divided the rest of the world into two basic categories – enemies and people they hadn't met yet. The few allies the Athenians possessed were temporary partners of convenience, with each side prepared to betray the other as soon as it became expedient to do so.

Yet this warlike city was the Athens that later ages were to revere; the city of Socrates, Sophocles and Euripides, where ground-breaking innovations in philosophy, architecture and the arts happened almost annually. At this time one could barely throw a lump of marble in the agora without hitting one of the Athenians responsible for the very foundations of later Western European culture.

It would also be fair to say that contemporary Greeks regarded this explosion of energy with a mixture of awe and trepidation. This was because, as the Persian empire across the Aegean Sea had already discovered, Athenian enterprise also extended into the military sphere. Athens was an aggressive and expansionist power, and the Athenians were unconventional and ferocious fighters who swiftly overcame setbacks and ruthlessly exploited victories. Both Sophocles and Socrates, for example, were every bit at home on a battlefield as in a symposium. This made Athens very discomforting for the city's less dynamic neighbours.

A Corinthian ambassador complained:

You have no idea what it is like to have to fight the Athenians. The Athenian is an innovator. He rapidly decides what to do, and does it just as quickly … He dares to attempt more than his resources allow, and remains confident even during the subsequent crisis ... While you [Spartans] hesitate, they always plunge right in. You stay at home, they are always abroad, because they think that the greater the distance, the larger the reward. If they win a victory, they follow it up at once, if defeated, they hardly fall back at all ...

If they set their minds on something and do not get it, they act as though they were deprived of something entitled to them. Then they immediately start looking for a different way to make good on their desires. If on the other hand, they do get what they want, they immediately regard it as a stepping-stone to something much greater.

With them, action follows ambition so closely that you might almost say that they get something as soon as they want it. Yet they never enjoy what they have, because they spend their lives enduring danger and difficulty to get more. And no matter how frantic or exhausting it might be, doing whatever has to be done to get what they want is their idea of a holiday.

To summarize – these people are congenitally incapable of either living in peace and quiet or of letting anyone else do so.

Thuc. 1.70

The Persian wars – where it all began
The traits described by the Corinthian ambassador had been amply demonstrated by the Athenians for most of the preceding century and the Corinthians, along with the Boeotians, Arcadians and Spartans, to name but a few, were heartily sick of it.

Athens had become top dog in Greece thanks to the Persians. In the previous century the fast-growing Persian empire had conquered the eastern shores of the Aegean Sea. The Greek cities of Ionia (roughly the western Aegean islands and the seaboard of modern Turkey) began the fifth century BC by rebelling against their Persian overlords. Athens enthusiastically supported the revolt, partly because Athens claimed leadership of the Ionians, who were allegedly descendants of a legendary Athenian king called Ion. The Athenians inspired an expedition to inland Asia Minor, which succeeded in burning down the Persian provincial capital of Sardis.

Up to this point, Persia had done nothing to the Athenians. Indeed, the Persians were barely aware that Athens existed. So both the Persian provincial governor and his sovereign, Darius, the Persian King of Kings, took deep offence at this unwonted aggression by a tiny upstart state from beyond their frontiers.

Nothing was done immediately. Darius was master of the largest empire in the world to date and had military business elsewhere. Nevertheless, seeing to Athens was high on the king's agenda. To keep it there, a slave was instructed to remind his royal master every day at dinner 'O King, remember the Athenians'.[2]

Once the Ionian revolt had been duly crushed, Darius followed up on these reminders. Starting with the island of Naxos, the Persians methodically subjugated their way westward through the Cyclades. Eventually, they conquered Euboea, an island across the strait from Attica. By now it was amply clear that Athens had provoked the Persians into undertaking the conquest of all Greece.

A Persian ambassador had already come to Sparta demanding that Sparta give earth and water as tokens of submission. Not unexpectedly, the Spartans told the emissary to get his own water and earth, and threw him down a well to find them. Nevertheless, many in the city probably held Athens responsible for provoking the entire crisis. Consequently, when a messenger arrived from Athens to say that the city expected to be invaded at any moment, the Spartans replied that help would be slow in coming.[3]

The Persian host had landed at Marathon, a wide sandy bay to the north east of Athens. With the help of a small contingent from the nearby city of Plataea, the Athenian army was blocking the exits from the beach. No one expected the Persians to sportingly refrain from hostilities until the Spartans eventually turned up.

So with the odds stacked at roughly 20–1 and any hope of immediate reinforcements gone, the Athenians did what anyone who knew them better might have expected. They attacked. In fact, they attacked at a flat-out run, which was not something that armies of the time were supposed to do. This surprised the archers who made up the bulk of the Persian force and the first volley of arrows perforated nothing but sand some distance behind the charging Greeks. There was no second volley, because by then the Athenian hoplites were on top of the bowmen. The ensuing combat proved that when a few heavily armed and desperate hoplites meet a mass of lightly armoured archers, quantity is no substitute for quality.

The epic victory at Marathon in 490 BC was a massive boost for Athenian prestige. It gave the Athenians a military reputation approaching that of the Spartans, and gave the world a long-distance foot race. The messenger who ran to Sparta and back with the unhelpful response then took part in the battle. Afterwards he sprinted the final 20 miles back to Athens with news of the victory. Having given the glad tidings, he promptly died, secure in the knowledge that he had impressed even a city of consummate over-achievers.

Marathon was the opening clash in a series of conflicts known today as the Persian Wars. Darius was unable to respond to the defeat, partly because lost Persian prestige inspired a series of revolts elsewhere. By 480, when Darius's successor Xerxes (Ḫšayāršā to his Persian subjects) was ready to resume where his father had left off, he found that the Greeks had largely united against him in an alliance called the Peloponnesian League. This was led by the Spartans, who were now prepared to fight, and comprehensively proved it at Thermopylae, where Leonidas and his heroic 300 held back the entire Persian army for three days.

The self-sacrifice of Leonidas allowed time for Athens to be evacuated. Nothing but empty buildings and stripped temples awaited the Persians, who took their vengeance on everything that could be burned or demolished. The people of Athens had taken to the sea, and when the Persians tried to follow them, their fleet was defeated at Salamis.

While the battered Persian ships withdrew to Mycale to patch their wounds, the Persian army retreated to Plataea in Boeotia. There the Persians were confronted by the largest combined army ever assembled in Greece. By coincidence, rather than a planned combined forces operation, the afternoon of the same day in August 479 BC saw the army demolish the Persian land forces while the Greek fleet did the same to the ships. The Persian invasion of Greece was literally an epic failure.

The Delian League

Before the Persians attacked, Athens had but an average navy. However, in 482 BC the city discovered what the later historian Xenophon called 'a divine bounty' – a huge and apparently inexhaustible vein of silver at Laurion, on the east coast of Attica. This bonanza gave the Athenians the most solid currency in Greece, and coins stamped with the owl of Athena soon became the currency against which other coinages were judged (and generally found wanting).

Rather than sit back and enjoy their good luck, the Athenians demonstrated exactly the sort of energy and enterprise that so upset the Corinthian ambassador. The money was invested in a large battle fleet of triremes, kitted out with the best that contemporary technology could provide. It was these ships that fought at Salamis, and these ships were at the spearhead of the force that destroyed the Persian fleet at Mycale. Unbeknownst to the rest of Greece, it was also the fleet with which Athens would build an empire.

Unlike the Athenians, the Spartans were a naturally conservative people. They had no great wish to continue fighting once the Persians had been forcibly ejected from the Greek mainland. Though practically invincible on the battlefield, the Spartan army was not large. And while that army was far from home, the Spartans fretted that their serf population of helots might rise in rebellion. There was good reason for this fear, for the Spartans brutally oppressed their helots, who hated them heartily in return.

As it happened, not only did the Spartans want their army back, but the rest of the Greeks strongly wanted them to have it. The difference between the Spartan lifestyle of his homeland and the relative decadence of Ionia had gone to the army commander's head. The man had discovered a very un-Spartan taste for luxury and wealth and had few scruples about how he helped himself to either. Since he retained the Spartan characteristics of abruptness, arrogance and dogmatism, this left him with few redeeming features. By popular request, he and his army were recalled,[4] and the Spartans neither offered nor were asked for replacements.

Without Sparta, the Peloponnesian League became defunct. Most who wanted to continue the war were Ionian, and Athens was in any case their *de facto* leader, so by default leadership of the war fell to Athens. The spiritual centre of the Ionian people was Delos. Here, on the sacred island birthplace of Artemis and Apollo, the Ionians had gathered since time immemorial for their folk festivals. So the Ionians repaired to Delos, there to form a new alliance known today as the Delian League.

The Delian League originally had three purposes: to prosecute the war against Persia; divide up any spoils of that war; and co-ordinate a response if Persia threatened to invade again. 'Hellenic treasurers' appointed by Athens assessed each state for its contribution to the war.

In 477 BC the league consisted of more or less equal partners in a voluntary confederacy. It was true that the war with Persia had by now subsided into the occasional violent skirmish, but this was arguably because the very existence of the confederacy restrained Persian aggression. Therefore, if contributions to the league kept them free and at relative peace, members felt it was a price worth paying.

In fact, membership grew slightly easier after a helpful offer from Athens. Since many island states had limited reserves of ships and manpower, providing these for the league was an onerous task. Athens had abundant ships and soldiers, so any city could let Athens provide their ships and manpower in return for a cash payment.

The Athenian empire is born

The first shadow fell over this happy arrangement when it was pointed out that the city of Carystus on the island of Euboea was not in the league. Euboea (as history had demonstrated) was a convenient staging post for the invasion of Attica, so the league had to defend it anyway. In effect, Carystus had a free ride on security.

Ambassadors came twice to Carystus bearing invitations for that city to join the Delian League. Each time Carystus asked why it should pay for protection it was already getting for free. In 472 BC the answer arrived. It took the form of the Athenian fleet and a swarm of hoplites. The Carystians promptly confessed themselves persuaded of the benefits and immediately joined the League. They were probably not the League's first involuntary members – considerable pressure had also been applied to cities on the coast of Asia Minor – but this was the first coercion applied to a city far from the front line.

Another turning point came the following year. Naxos in the Cyclades islands was a founder member of the League. The city contributed ships and manpower, but had become increasingly dissatisfied with a war that was doing little for Naxos, but much for the benefit of Athens. The Athenians responded that there was not a lot the Naxians could do, as joining the League had been an irrevocable commitment. Naxos withdrew anyway.

It took a substantial siege before the Naxians changed their minds. It appears that the city walls of Naxos were torn down to prevent similar disagreements in future. While they were at it, the Athenians confiscated the city's fleet and demanded a monetary membership contribution henceforth.

During the next decade Athens continued to expand its control over the League and to force member states to co-operate with Athenian aims. That co-operation did not extend far in the other direction. This was made abundantly clear to the people of Thasos, a League city that had become wealthy in part from gold mines in nearby Thrace.

To Thasian dismay, the Athenians disputed the ownership of certain gold mines and began to force their way into markets on the Thracian mainland, which the Thasians had always considered their own. When Thasos protested by threatening to leave the League, Athens responded with the now-standard invasion force. Thasos appealed to Sparta for help, but before Sparta could act, a devastating earthquake crippled the country. The helots saw this as an opportunity to rise in rebellion. Not only was Sparta unable to aid Thasos but the Spartans had to make a humiliating appeal to Athens for military support.

The Spartans later repented of their offer and asked the Athenians to leave again, but Sparta's reputation was so damaged that a former ally, the city of Megara, volunteered to join the League. This infuriated the Corinthians, who had hopes of making Megara a satellite state, but for the moment there was little Corinth could do. Meanwhile, Thasos was duly subjugated, and to no one's surprise a league court awarded Athens the Thasian assets in mainland Thrace. A colony – Amphipolis – was established on the mainland to hammer home the point of Athenian dominance. Like Naxos, Thasos also lost its navy, and thereafter was forced to pay for the maintenance of the very ships that subjugated it.

It was becoming plain to even the most self-deluding members of the League that the 'equal partnership' to which they had signed up was gone. Their confederacy had somehow morphed into what some Athenians were openly calling their 'empire', and the purpose of that empire was not the defeat of Persia but the aggrandizement of Athens.

The next step came in 454 BC, when the league voted to move its treasury from Delos to the 'greater security' of Athens. By now Athens had garrisons 'protecting' many of the smaller cities. Being under what was in effect military occupation, these smaller cities took their voting orders from Athens. The league treasury had a substantial surplus of 9,000 talents of gold, for even as the war had been winding down, assessments for contributions (now redefined as tribute) had been creeping up.

Pericles, the Athenian leader, had an idea of what to do with the surplus cash. The League had been founded to mitigate Persian aggression. Therefore the current financial surplus should be used to undo the damage that Persian aggression had already wrought. The Ionians were a god-fearing folk, so temples ravaged by the Persians should be the first priority of a League-financed re-building project. This should be done one city at a time, and where better to start than Athens?

One of the many the temples rebuilt (with no expense spared) was on the Acropolis. It is a sad irony that the Parthenon, one of the greatest architectural expressions of the human spirit, was built on contributions extorted by Athens from former allies who had become subjects.

At least the Athenian empire was no grim tyranny. Many Ionians voluntarily made their way to Athens to revel in the sheer dynamism of a state that questioned everything and believed that anything was possible. Even as far back as the 490s an exile from the isle of Lesbos had reduced his audience to tears with *The Fall of Miletos*, the heart-rending play about the reconquest of his rebel city by the Persians. Many others had followed, including

Herodotus of Halicarnassus, whose account of the Persian wars is the world's first work of history. And Athens might despotically rule the League, but the city itself was a democracy.

Democracy was a new concept. The rest of the world was still coming to grips with the idea of citizens coming together and deciding the fate of their city in the market place. The Persians reportedly fell about with laughter when informed that the Athenians actually did things that way. Even in Athens many had reservations, and since the doubters were the propertied literary class, this is why even today we call it 'democracy', meaning in the original Greek something like 'mob rule' rather than 'rule by the people', which would be 'demarchy'.

Unsurprisingly, the Athenian experiment made tyrants and oligarchs everywhere rather uneasy, all the more so as the democratic experiment was proving both durable and successful. In fact, even the Persians allowed democracies in those Greek cities they had reconquered, since it did not stop their newly regained subjects from paying taxes and voting apparently kept them happy. In Athens anyone who wanted could lead the empire[5] simply by standing up in the assembly and making a proposal sufficiently agreeable to his fellow voters. Athens did have appointed officials (these were chosen by lottery from a pool of qualified citizens), but the officials were there to make sure that assembly meetings were orderly and held on time. The officials did not make policy.

The world according to Pericles

In fact, policy was generally made by Pericles, who had so recently decided to appropriate the League treasury for an Athenian building programme. Like any contemporary politician, Pericles was technically no more than an ordinary Athenian with a big mouth, but in fact he ran the city – a performance that was all the more masterly because he had no more right than the next man to do so. A comic poet said of Pericles:

> He had a tongue that could argue both sides [of an argument] with irresistible fury ...[6]

In appearance, Pericles was said to somewhat resemble Pisistratus, the tyrant whose sons had been replaced by the vigorous and turbulent democracy of Athens. In this democracy anyone taking the part of a despot or autocrat could expect short shrift. Athens practised ostracism, a sort of reverse election, which exiled the 'winner' from the city for ten years. Pericles not only avoided this fate, but used his popular appeal to inflict it on his opponents. He ruled not by the power of his office but by the force of his personality:

> He could generally persuade the people to follow him, consenting by their own free will to what he had demonstrated by clear argument had to be done. At other times he urged a course of policy and forced it through against popular opposition, so that finally, whether they liked it or not, the people ended up doing what was good for them.[7]

Pericles was a consummate politician. He had to be when every policy initiative was voted on by the entire male population of the city, and so basically required a referendum to pass. Apart from Thucydides, who greatly admired Pericles, we have little direct information about the man until a biography by Plutarch from half a millennium later. However, in the Pericles described by Thucydides, modern historians have noted a disconnect between the politician's words and his policies.

When reproached for annexing the funds of the Delian League for building work in Athens, Pericles had a defence ready. It was Athens that was the shield and sword of the Ionian people, and it was the ships and men of Athens that kept Persia at bay. The rest of the league (with a few exceptions, which still contributed troops) paid for this service with money. It was decades since the Persians had been a serious threat, and therefore, ipso facto, Athens was keeping its part of the contract. If Athens could defend the other league cities for less than the contracted price for the service, no one had any right to complain how the difference was spent.

Athens, declared Pericles, was at the heart of all that was honest and good in Greece.

> Our love of beauty does not lead to extravagance, and our fondness for intellectual activity does not make us soft. For us, wealth is something to be put to work, not something to boast about ... when a man is not interested in politics, we do not say he minds his own business – we say that he has no business being here at all. We Athenians decide our affairs for ourselves, or submit them for discussion ... and we make our friends by doing things for them, not by receiving favours from them. When we do kindness to others we do it spontaneously, without reckoning whether we will profit or lose by it. In summary, I do declare that our city is an education to the rest of Greece.
>
> Thuc. 2.40

As for their empire, the Athenians had nothing to apologize for. They were aware that the power of their city was making the rest of Greece uneasy, and whenever they had the chance, they defended themselves in inter-city assemblies. Here an ambassador puts the Athenian case.

> After the threat from Persia, we looked to our own honour and self-interest. And once it turned out that we were surrounded by enemies, and had to crush some revolts, and it was plain that you [Peloponnesians] had turned against us ... well, there was no point in letting our empire go, especially as our former allies would just go straight over to your side ... We have done nothing unusual, for it is certainly human nature for a people to accept an empire when it drops into their laps. And naturally we refuse to give it up; for those three very good reasons [given above] security, honour and self-interest ... It has always been the rule that the weak are subservient to the strong ... and no strong people have ever rejected the opportunity of expansion that their superior strength offers.
>
> Thuc. 1.76

What was remarkable about the Athenians, the ambassadors insisted, was that they were such moderate overlords.

> Being human, [we] enjoy our position of power, yet pay far more attention to the demands of justice than our circumstances force us to. If you really wanted to see how moderate we are, just imagine what anyone else would do in our position ... Unlike other imperial powers, which simply consider that might is right, our subjects are accustomed to us treating them as equals. So when they think they are hard done by in a court case, or when we use the power our empire gives us, they feel no gratitude for the privileges that we have let them keep. Instead they get more agitated about the small differences between us and them than they would get if we just set the law aside and openly exploited them.
>
> Ibid.

The position of Pericles and the Athenians was that their city had become foremost in Greece through the virtue of its people. They implied that Sparta was jealous of the growing power of Athens and that Peloponnesian paranoia was causing the states of mainland Greece to unfairly gang up on them. Athenian dominance of Ionia was simply a natural consequence of

Athenian leadership and power, and if their subjects resented this it was because they were ungrateful for the degree of liberty that the Athenians – out of the goodness of their hearts – allowed them to have.

Thucydides does not hide that his Athens was both dynamic and imperial. He portrays the city's spokesmen as positively revelling in the fact. That Athens was also expansionist is because its strategic situation forced the city to be so. The looming threat of war in the near future was caused by the fear and resentment of the Peloponnesian states.

That this fear and resentment was due to Athens picking city states off one by one as the opportunity had presented itself is not mentioned. Nor, given the vaunted Athenian energy and ambition, can any convincing reason be given why Athens would suddenly decide it had enough subjects and power and abandon further expansion. Therefore, states not already absorbed by the Athenian empire were quite justified for feeling that if they did not get together and do something about Athens, sooner or later Athens would do something about them.

430 BC: war!

Thucydides has Pericles not merely outline but describe in detail how Athens planned to deal with the threat from Sparta and allied states. This is consistent with Athenian policy, because as Pericles explained, most states preparing for war expelled foreigners to keep secret their strength and intentions. Athens, on the other hand, wanted any potential attackers to know exactly what they were letting themselves in for. Foreign observers were welcome.

The cornerstone of Athenian strategy was sea power. 'We must learn to think of our city as an island,' Pericles told the citizens. This was hard for many Athenians to come to terms with, as at that time many Athenians did not live in Athens and in fact rarely visited the city. These citizens lived in the demes of Attica, towns and villages with their own customs and social structure. However, Athens could not defend the demes against Sparta's unbeatable army. Therefore Pericles' policy was not to try. As he noted, it was hard for an army to sustain itself away from home for any length of time, and the Spartans simply did not have the resources to do this.

Certainly the Spartans and their allies could invade Attica once a year. Certainly they could devastate the crops and the harvest. Yet as modern research has demonstrated, it is one thing to devastate a crop, another to devastate the underlying infrastructure. It takes a lot of work to put a vineyard or olive grove permanently out of commission. Trees have to be chopped down, and vine roots grubbed up. Even then, rebuilding and replanting can make good the damage within a few years, and there was a lot of Attica to devastate. Furthermore, all that devastation would be essentially unproductive. For over a generation Athens had imported its grain and other essential foods. As Pericles pointed out, there was no way the Spartans could stop this: 'That takes a navy, and they are farmers.'

Today there is a certain scepticism that Athens was really set on fighting the war by pulling itself tortoise-like behind the city walls and waiting for the enemy to go away. Such a strategy was utterly unlike the Athens its neighbours knew and hated. There is a strong possibility that what Thucydides describes as a carefully contrived defensive strategy was in fact an ad hoc response to an unexpected crisis – the plague.

Where this plague came from is uncertain. One suspect is Egypt, where the Athenians had recently made a determined attempt to establish a bridgehead in Persian-occupied territory. The Athenian invasion had been thrown back with heavy casualties, but links with Egypt remained strong. Certainly the fact that the plague first took hold in the Piraeus suggests that it came from abroad. Within Athens, the plague was devastating. The Spartans did indeed invade, and the population of Attica was jammed within the city walls, where – oddly enough, if Pericles had long planned for this – little had been arranged by way of accommodation for them. The shanty towns in a city that could easily hold off the most powerful army in Greece were defenceless against microbes.

> The doctors could not do much, because they did not know what to do. In fact, because they were most exposed to infection, many of them were among the first to die. Art and science were equally useless in finding a remedy. Praying at the temples and consulting oracles likewise failed, and eventually people were so overwhelmed by their suffering that they didn't even bother to try.
>
> Thuc 2.52

The plague not only devastated the population of Athens, but also weakened the social fabric:

> The laws of god and man alike lost their force. The good died just like the bad, so it made no difference whether one worshipped the gods or not. And no one expected to live long enough to be brought to trial and

punished – the general sentiment was that everyone was under sentence
of death in any case.

Thuc 2.53

If Pericles had been contemplating offensive action, the plague killed any
such intention as effectively as it slaughtered the Athenians themselves. The
Athenians were not even able to help their only ally at Marathon, the little
city of Plataea, which the Spartans now besieged. The plague also deprived
Athens of the helmsman who had guided the city smoothly to its current
ascendency in Greece. Pericles first lost his sons to the plague, then in 429
he himself perished.

Before the plague hit, Athenian offensive operations had begun in Thrace,
far to the north-east and not coincidentally in the opposite direction from
Sparta in the south-west. (And this is a hint of what the planned Athenian
strategy might in fact have been.) Once the plague took hold the Athenian
offensive lost traction. Fresh troops from Athens brought the plague with
them, and effectively devastated the armies they were supposed to be
reinforcing. This lack of success brought Alexander, Macedon's fickle and
opportunistic king, temporarily over to the Spartan side.

Success came mainly at sea, thanks to the enterprising Athenian admiral
Phormio. Part of the reason for Phormio's success was because he kept his
rowers well away from contamination. In fact, the Athenian navy gave
plague-riddled Piraeus such a wide berth that the harbour was nearly
captured by a Peloponnesian surprise attack. Athenian difficulties with the
plague also gave the people of Mytilene on the island of Lesbos the chance
to realize their long-nurtured desire of leaving the Delian League.

This Athens simply could not tolerate. If the rebellion of Mytilene
succeeded, the rest of the empire would quickly unravel. Every effort was
made to force Mytilene into submission at all costs. Sparta promised to
send help to Mytilene, but mobilized their men with such typical Spartan
sluggishness that Mytilene had run out of food before they arrived. Faced
with starvation, the rebels threw themselves on the mercy of their
besiegers.

By now the war had been underway for four years. It was candidly
admitted that fear of Athens had long ago replaced fear of Persia as the reason
that the Delian League remained in being. A passionate debate now took
place in the Athenian assembly about what fate for Mytilene would most
effectively terrorize the cities of the confederacy into remaining committed
to the Athenian cause.

In the end, the Athenians decided to kill the thousand Mytilenians they held most responsible for the revolt, enslave the rest, destroy the city walls and divide the land of the island among themselves. This was a milder version of their earlier plan, urged by Cleon (with the quote that starts this chapter), that all male inhabitants of the island should be put to the sword and only the wives and children enslaved.

The milder version only squeaked through the assembly in an amendment. This led to a frantic dash across the Aegean by the ship carrying news of the change in plans, since a trireme bearing orders to perpetrate the massacre had left the previous day. However, the ship countermanding those orders travelled so fast that it arrived in the harbour of Mytilene while the Athenian commander was still working out how to implement the mass execution.

If the Athenians were relatively merciful with Mytilene, the Spartans were as grimly merciless as ever. They finally captured little Plataea, although most of the garrison managed to slip away beforehand. Those who remained were asked the simple question: 'What have you done to help the Spartans?' Since no one could provide a satisfactory answer, the defenders were executed and their womenfolk enslaved.

Pylos 425 BC

By the sixth year of the war something of a pattern had developed. The Spartans and their allies would march on Attica. They would spend a while devastating some cropland and admiring the formidable Long Walls of Athens. These walls stretched four-and-a-half miles from the city to the sea, and were so effortlessly superior to the finest efforts of contemporary siege technology that the Spartans did not even try assailing them. Behind the walls carts laden with foodstuffs trundled from harbour to market, making the Spartans' attack on the Athenian harvest good for little but relieving their frustration. Then the Spartans would go home.

While the Spartans were typically predictable, equally typically the Athenians were not. One of the things they could do with a large navy was unload an army almost anywhere on the coast of mainland Greece. Since nowhere in mainland Greece was more than 60 miles from the sea, no one knew where the Athenians were going to strike next, and no Spartan ally was safe. Nor, indeed, was Sparta.

The Spartans discovered this in the spring of 425 BC, once their army had set out on its annual commute to the Athenian fields. While this army was having a miserable time trampling down green corn in heavy seasonal rain, the Athenians made themselves at home on the tiny island of Pylos (modern Navarino) on the south-west Peloponnese. They even fortified a suitable piece of the mainland opposite. The city of Sparta was a set of small communities in the valley of a river at the foot of Mount Taygetus. Famously, it had no defensive walls,[8] so the discovery that the Athenians were much closer to their homes[9] than they were caused the Spartan army considerable concern. Though only a fortnight into their annual pillage, they precipitately abandoned the event and hurried home.

On arriving, they were startled to discover that the impertinent Athenians did not embark and sail off as they usually did. Instead, a rabble of light Athenian troops and skirmishers coolly awaited the inevitable assault. This was spearheaded by the cream of Sparta's invincible hoplite army, which speedily took over the island. This proved to be a misjudgement, since once the hoplites were on Pylos there was no way of getting them off. Between themselves and the mainland a squadron of Athenian triremes patrolled like sharks, and not a hoplite wanted to venture on to the water. Repeated attempts by Spartan ships to break the blockade were foiled by superior Athenian seamanship.

There was some debate by the Athenian assembly about how to deal with the Spartans stranded on the island until Cleon, the would-be butcher of Mytilene, undertook to deal with the matter personally. He was intelligent enough to co-opt one Demosthenes as a fellow general. The landing at Pylos had originally been Demosthenes' idea, and since then Demosthenes had been thinking hard about how to cope with Spartan hoplites.

The Spartans had been expecting anything but a direct military assault, since no one in their right minds voluntarily attacked them. Consequently, the Athenians over-ran the Spartan pickets and established a beachhead before the surprised hoplites could rally. Once they did, the Spartans expected that the coming fight would be one-sided. They had superior armour, training and equipment. It should have been a short fight, except that the superior armour and equipment were heavy, and the Athenians surrounded the Spartans with a swarm of bowmen and lightly armed javelineers:

There was no single group to counter-attack. If the Spartans charged forward, they were shot at from the rear. If they turned on the enemy on one flank, their backs were exposed to the other. Wherever they went, the enemy were behind them. Their arrows, stones, javelins and slingshots were highly effective at long range. It was impossible to bring the fighting to short-range, for the enemy skipped easily away, and came back as soon as their opponents stopped for a breather.

Thuc. 4.32

It turned out that the Athenians had more missiles than the Spartans had stamina, so in the end it was indeed a one-sided fight. Being Spartans, the hoplites were prepared to fight to the death, but it was hard to make a famous last stand against an enemy who kept running away. It was an approach to warfare that the Spartan army had never encountered before. After pondering it for several hours, under a steady hailstorm of missiles, the Spartans came up with an unprecedented move of their own. They surrendered.

This development sent shock waves through Greece. As Thucydides has a Spartan remark, 'When Dorians fight Ionians, the Dorians usually win.'[10] And when the Dorians were Spartan, the result should be inevitable. The Spartans did not lose battles, and in the highly improbable event that they did, the idea that they might surrender was almost inconceivable. And these were not just any Spartans – as mentioned above, these were the cream of the army, representing some of the top families in the state. There were many in Sparta who felt that their city had been dragged into the war by cities like Corinth, which were prepared to be rabidly belligerent so long as it was Spartans who did the actual fighting. For these people, this setback was the last straw in a war that was going nowhere. Ambassadors went to Athens to ask for their hoplites back and to inquire how the Athenians felt about making peace.

But the Athenians were on a roll. As the Corinthian ambassador had warned, the Athenian approach to success was to regard it as a stepping stone to yet greater accomplishments. Since the setback to Sparta had cowed the unwilling allies of Athens, Cleon increased the Athenian war-chest by doubling the tribute. Then the Athenians launched a series of commando-style raids on the Spartan coast. The Spartans could not garrison every outpost, as this would leave them too thinly stretched to mount an effective defence anywhere. Alternatively, a concentrated force would be formidable, but would arrive at any crisis well after Athenian raiders had gone, in effect leaving the outposts undefended. Nevertheless, the Spartans opted for the latter, somewhat to the disappointment of the Athenians. Having given their opponents a bloody nose at Pylos, they were keen to see if the process could be repeated elsewhere.

The answer, as the campaigns of 424 in northern Greece clearly demonstrated, was essentially 'no'. The Spartans on Pylos had been foiled because they had neither light infantry of their own nor, better yet, cavalry, which would have massacred the light troops as they pulled back. Brasidas was the most warlike of the remaining Spartan leaders, and blessed with a very un-Spartan ability to learn from experience. His army contained a large element of helots, presumably recruited to provide the light troops so significantly lacking on the island.

Brasidas intended to roll back Athenian advances in Thrace. It did not matter that most cities in the region just wanted both warring factions to go away. 'We Spartans are justified in liberating you against your will because it is for your own good,' Brasidas informed the surly Acanthians,[11] and proceeded to apply this policy across the region. Fighting continued around Athens' new colony of Amphipolis for the next two years. To the eternal benefit of posterity Brasidas finally captured the Athenian colony. This capture meant that the Athenian commanding the relief force was made a scapegoat and exiled. His exit from the war meant that the commander, none other than our Thucydides, could concentrate on the serious business of writing history.

Spartan success at Amphipolis had another unintended consequence. It brought Cleon north to oppose Brasidas, and in the subsequent fighting both men were killed. Cleon and Brasidas had been the cheerleaders for their respective cities' war parties, and the pair had practically worked in tandem to scupper an earlier ceasefire worked out in 423. Once the two had finally cancelled each other out, peacemakers on both sides breathed a sigh of relief and set about hammering out a treaty. This agreement was known as the Peace of Nicias, after the Athenian general Nicias, its main proponent.

The Spartans intended the agreement to bring an end to almost a decade of continual warfare. The Athenians intended it to allow them to resume picking off Greek cities one-by-one without the bother of having to fight the Spartans for them. These mismatching viewpoints did not bode well for the future.

Chapter 2

From Melos to Sicily

Saying that you have never done us any harm is not going to stop us ...
the fact is that the strong do what they have the power to do, and the
weak suffer what they must.

Athenian general to the leaders of Melos (Thuc. 5.85ff.)

Alcibiades

Among the Athenian politicians who opposed the peace treaty was an up-and-coming young man called Alcibiades. Alcibiades had nothing against peace with Sparta, but if a treaty was going to be made, he felt that he should be the one making it. Cleon, though probably a more substantial figure than the blustering demagogue Thucydides makes him out to be, had been a poor successor to Pericles. Alcibiades reckoned that he could do better, not least because after his father was killed fighting the Thebans he had been brought up in the household of Pericles, to whom he was related.

The grandfather of Alcibiades had handled Spartan interests in Athens until his death. Alcibiades felt he should have that position now, and he was a young man accustomed to getting his way. Plutarch tells a story of when Alcibiades was a boy, playing at knucklebones in the street. Not only did he demand that passing traffic stop until he had finished, but when one cart driver insisted on driving on, Alcibiades threw himself flat in front of the cart and dared the driver to run him over.

This wilful attitude remained in his adulthood, when the antics of the young man alternately offended, delighted and scandalized the Athenians. Alcibiades was handsome, brilliant and in the words of Plutarch 'filled with vanity and wantonness'.[12] One Hipponicus could testify to this. He was a leading citizen whom Alcibiades once marched up to and sucker-punched while his companions fell about laughing. Alcibiades later explained that he had nothing against Hipponicus, but he had been dared to do it. On another occasion he mutilated a beautiful dog by cutting off its tail and remarked laughingly that he had done so because he wanted the Athenians to be talking about him for that misdeed, and nothing worse.

It was generally reckoned that Socrates had been the making of Alcibiades. As a handsome youth, the young aristocrat had his pick of wealthy lovers, most of whom he despised and made ridiculous. However, after he fell into a relationship with Socrates, Alcibiades curbed his earlier excesses and turned his flamboyant energies to politics.

In keeping with his self-proclaimed role as Sparta's representative in Athens, Alcibiades was solicitous to the needs of the Spartan captives from Pylos while they were imprisoned in the city. Despite the kudos that Alcibiades reckoned he should have earned from this, the Spartans turned to the older and more experienced Nicias when they came to make peace. After successful negotiations ended with a peace treaty, the popular catchphrase went round Athens that Pericles had got the city into the war and Nicias had got them out of it. This infuriated Alcibiades, and that the subsequent peace was called the 'Peace of Nicias' made him wild with envy. The young firebrand promptly turned his considerable energy and not inconsiderable talent to the task of ensuring that this peace did not last. There were others who felt the same way.

Peace in fifth-century Greece was in any case something of a relative term. Given that warfare was an integral part of life in a city state, one made peace to free up resources for fighting somewhere else. While Nicias had hammered out the best terms available, neither side really intended to honour those terms once they had got their prisoners back. Given that both Athens and Sparta had to some degree signed the treaty in bad faith, the odds inevitably favoured those such as Alcibiades who wanted to give war a chance.

Sparta's allies were outraged that their champion had stopped fighting and stung by the Spartan retort that none of the allies had ever really started. Thebes and Corinth were among those who rejected the peace terms outright, and indeed, Corinth was only prevented from taking matters further by swift diplomacy, which joined Athens and Sparta in a defensive pact. The prospect of taking on the combined force of the two most powerful nations of Greece was also enough to restrain the Thebans, though barely. The Thebans ended up negotiating a ceasefire with Athens that had to be renewed every ten days.

The calumny that the Corinthians talked a good war but preferred someone else to do the actual fighting was given added heft by the next Corinthian diplomatic initiative. As a neighbour in the Peloponnese, Argos had a long tradition of warfare with Sparta, and had not done too badly at it, given Sparta's famed military prowess.

The last round of Argive/Spartan hostilities had been a generation ago in 446 when Athens, Argos and their allies had butted heads with the Spartans in a brief and inconclusive war. This had resulted in a thirty-year peace treaty between Argos and Sparta, which had actually lasted the course, perhaps because the Spartans had been otherwise occupied since 431. Now the last days of the treaty were ticking down like the timer on a bomb, and few doubted that Argos and Sparta would be at war soon after the treaty finally expired.

The Corinthians hated the Athenians, who had used the war to take over formerly Corinthian allies and colonies, especially in the north-west of Greece. Yet Corinth had now also developed a grudge against the Spartans, whom they called 'the common enemy of the Peloponnese'. When Argos had its inevitable clash with Sparta, the Corinthians wanted the Argives to know that they would be right behind them. The Argives themselves made it public to potential allies that they were open to suggestions. Their own city had profited from its neutrality in the most recent round of fighting, and Sparta's reputation was now at a low ebb. In Athens, Alcibiades scented an opportunity.

Athens had already returned to its predatory ways and picked off the city of Scione, an ex-member of the Delian League that had seen the arrival of Brasidas in their part of northern Greece as an opportunity to rebel. Once peace was made with Sparta, the Athenians promptly assaulted Scione, reproachfully killed the town's menfolk and enslaved everyone else. They then resettled the place with survivors of the Spartan massacre at Plataea.[13]

Mantinea 418 BC

This and other breaches of the peace led to Sparta dispatching a delegation to Athens. Despite Athenian aggression on a number of fronts, the Spartans were in a conciliatory mood. The open-house approach of Argos to potential allies had struck an anti-Spartan nerve in the rest of Greece and offers to collaborate in taking the Spartans down a peg came thick and fast. The Corinthians were in, as were the cities of Tegea and Mantinea. The city of Elis in Arcadia followed, as did some Greek cities in Thrace, which had less than fond memories of Brasidas. Feeling somewhat alone in an unfriendly world, Sparta's main ambition was to make sure that the peace with Athens remained intact.

The delegation came at a good time for Nicias, who had been relentlessly hounded by Alcibiades in the assembly over every stumble in the highly imperfect peace process. The Spartans assured the Athenian council that they came with full powers to negotiate whatever terms would allow the two cities to maintain a just and equitable peace.

Alcibiades took the Spartan delegates aside after this meeting and warned them that they should under no circumstances reveal to the full assembly of the Athenian people what they had told the council. Alcibiades averred that the assembly was an unpredictable beast. If the people found that the delegates had the power to negotiate anything up to a complete new treaty, they would take advantage of the fact to demand major concessions in the new terms.

The Spartans took this advice and duly informed the assembly that any major issues would have to be referred to Sparta. They were completely nonplussed when Alcibiades then addressed the people and informed them that the Spartans were obviously not serious about keeping the peace if their delegation had no powers to negotiate properly. Nicias later tried to repair the damage, but Alcibiades and his supporters had their next question ready. Thebes had refused to comply with the terms of the treaty, and even now peace was maintained by a fragile ceasefire. Would Sparta renounce her erstwhile ally, and if not, how could Sparta complain if Athens followed the national trend and allied with Argos?

When Sparta refused to abandon Thebes, Alcibiades put the motion to the Athenian assembly that the Argive alliance should go ahead, and the treaty was duly made. As a further sign of Sparta's increasing isolation, Spartan athletes were denied access to the Olympic games of the year, since the organizers claimed that the Spartans had failed to pay a fine imposed earlier.

Interested neutrals, including the still-exiled Thucydides, watched to see how Sparta would react to being out-manoeuvred by the more diplomatically nimble Alcibiades. The Argive alliance had shredded the already tattered peace with Sparta, but mainly thanks to the efforts of Nicias, the shreds still hung together. Athens was not openly at war with Sparta, although the situation in the Peloponnese was deteriorating by the day.

For the Spartans, the crunch came when they received word from their allies in the city of Tegea that the city was about to join the Argive alliance. Tegea was strategically significant as it controlled the valleys leading from Laconia, so the Spartans had made considerable efforts to keep the city loyal to their cause. If Tegea did join with Argos, it was plain that unless a stand was made soon, the Spartans would be left without an ally in the peninsula. There is also a suggestion, which is now impossible to confirm or deny, that it was at this time that the Spartans found a new friend. There was every reason to keep this friendship secret, for this new friend (if this was indeed the case) was none other than the common enemy of all Greeks – Persia.

By now the Persians had brought themselves fully up to speed with affairs on the Greek mainland and had decided that the conservative Spartans had little taste for a military adventure against Persia. On the other hand, since the Athenians were ready, willing and perfectly able to make a considerable nuisance of themselves to both states, Persia and Sparta found that they shared some common ground. Possibly at this point, and certainly at some time over the next decade, clandestine Persian assistance to Sparta became a major influence on events in Greece.

Thus in 418, quite possibly emboldened by Persian offers of assistance, and perhaps also fortified by a substantial Persian cash deposit as evidence of good faith, the Spartan army took to the field to persuade the Tegeans that defection was not in their best interest. Together with their allies, including an Athenian contingent, the Argives marched against the Spartans to defend Tegea's freedom of choice. The Argive army plus allies was quite possibly the strongest army fielded in Greece to date. So it was a pity that when it gave battle in the early autumn, the Spartans whipped it quite handily, settling the war and the question of the Tegean alliance in a single afternoon.

Fortunately for the Athenians, their contingent was not heavily involved in the battle, and while the Spartans were single-minded in crushing those who opposed them on the battlefield, they had little interest in their enemies once they started running away. However, the Argives suffered heavy casualties. The prestige of Alcibiades and his war party took an equally heavy hit. He and the Athenians had to endure humiliating setbacks through 417 as city states across Greece reconsidered matters in the light of Sparta's demonstration of continuing military superiority.

Yet even though Athenian cavalry had exchanged blows with Spartans on the battlefield, neither state had yet officially renounced the peace treaty.

Melos 416

Athenians in general, and Alcibiades in particular, were seldom deterred long by setbacks. If the Spartans had shown that they were basically unbeatable in a land battle, well, this was hardly news. But the Spartans were still rotten seamen, so perhaps it was time for the Athenians also to return to their core skills. It was time to pick off another island state and force it into their empire.

Melos is a small island of about 60 square miles, the most western isle of the Cyclades chain, which has Naxos near the other end. The name may come from the shape, which resembles an apple (Melo) from which a giant has taken a huge bite from the north-west. Later ages know it as the original home of the famed Venus di Milo, but to contemporaries it was a small and relatively unimportant island only of interest to those who collected the high-value pottery and obsidian pieces in which it specialized.

However, like most of the peoples of the southern Aegean, the Melians were Dorian. Indeed, many Greeks believed that Melos had been founded by colonists from Sparta itself. This meant that they were naturally sympathetic to Sparta in the same way that the Ionians were naturally pro-Athens. The Melians were well aware that any island supporting Sparta would attract the attention of the Athenian navy, and therefore tried to remain as inconspicuous as possible. Despite this, and despite its proclaimed neutrality, the island had been given a desultory plundering by the Athenian general Nicias in 426. This was probably the result of Athenian petulance that the island had declined an invitation to join the Delian League, even though the Melians had earlier been active in the war against Persia. However, a recently discovered inscription known as 'the Spartan War Fund' tells us that the Melians were among states that contributed financially to Sparta's war effort, though it cannot be certain whether this was a Melian response to Athenian aggression or the act that provoked that aggression in the first place.

Whatever the case, Athens had ignored Melos for a decade, and now suddenly, while ostensibly at peace with Sparta and her allies, launched a full-scale attack on the island. Some modern historians have alleged that the Melians were more overtly anti-Athenian than our sources tell us, but even if true in this regard, there were more deserving cases for Athenian attention. It is more probable that the sudden interest of Athens in Melos can be traced back directly to the debacle at Mantinea.

At Mantinea, Athens in general and Alcibiades in particular had lost prestige.[14] This loss was not just a blow to national pride (though to a people like the Athenians that blow was grievous enough), but also a sign of weakness, and this could not be tolerated in a nation that controlled its former allies by force alone. The Athenians freely admitted that in acquiring their empire in the way they had, they had taken a tiger by the tail. Letting go would be immediately fatal, and even any sign that their grip was weakening was a danger.

Yet there was little Melos, an independent island state, which could apparently ignore the Athenian superpower and remain peacefully neutral while political storms shook the rest of Greece. To the subject peoples of the Athenian island empire, the very weakness of the Melians was a call to rebellion. The population of Melos was about 3,000 in all. If the Athenians could not even bring Melos under their control, those contemplating rebellion mused that perhaps Athens might also fail to reincorporate a larger and better-defended island that opted out.

That the Melians had never done the Athenians any harm was irrelevant. Melos harmed their empire by simply existing, and thus showing other islands that such an existence was possible. Secondly, after Mantinea there was a need to demonstrate that Athens was still to be feared. Melos would provide that demonstration.

The attack on Melos was considered – both at the time and ever since – a flagrant injustice based purely on physical force. Even the ostensibly impartial Thucydides showed his outrage in a carefully crafted section of his history, which has since become known as 'The Melian dialogue'. This dialogue purports to be a conversation between the Melian leaders and the invading Athenian generals on the eve of their actual attack.[15]

The dialogue
The Athenians opened this discussion by saying that its only purpose was for the Melians to present a case for how they might save themselves and their city.

> We will not use purple prose about how we deserve our empire ... or that we are attacking you because of the wrongs you have done us. Nobody would believe it anyway ... In return, you should concentrate on getting what concessions you can, bearing in mind that we are far stronger than you.

All the Athenians wanted to know was if the Melians could think of any reason why sparing them would be good for Athens. The Melians suggested that perhaps setting a precedent of unprovoked aggression and unfairness might eventually come back to bite the Athenians if their fortunes should change.

The Athenians said that issues of fairness and justice were not relevant to the discussion.

> This is not a fair fight in which the winner gains honour and the loser is shamed. It's simply a question of whether you are going to give in to overwhelmingly superior force ... There's nothing disgraceful in giving way to the greatest state in Greece and becoming a tribute-paying state. Especially when you consider the alternative [which was death].

Unstated but implicit in the dialogue is the ironic fact that the Athenians had rejected this very argument when they refused to come to terms with Persia. Now, Athens was the overbearing bully, and one that did not have even the Persian excuse that it was attacked first.

Thucydides has two reasons for presenting this dialogue as he does. Firstly, it has been convincingly argued[16] that this dialogue shows Alcibiades and his war party at their ravening and immoral worst. This argument makes the justifiable claim that under the influence of Alcibiades and his war party Athens had lost its moral compass. The state that currently hosted Socrates and which Pericles had recently called 'the School of Hellas' could now come up with no better philosophy than 'might is right'.

Thucydides' second reason for presenting a dialogue that gives the Melians the moral high ground is to highlight another Athenian failing. For the Greeks, pride in oneself and one's achievements was right and good. Yet even the most florid boasts should acknowledge a debt to Fortune. There was supposed to be an awareness that her gifts could be withdrawn without notice, and some empathy with those not currently favoured. Proper pride contained a decent dose of humility – a humility completely lacking from the Athenian side of the dialogue. Thucydides shows the Athenians as having the type of pride the Greeks called *hubris*.

Hubris was what had made the Persian invaders bring a block of top-class stone with them to Greece. The intention was that after Persia's invading army had triumphed, the stone would be carved into an appropriate statue of victory, to be prominently displayed thereafter to remind the Greeks of their subject status.

There existed a particular goddess whose job it was to deal with *hubris*. Her name was Nemesis. To the Greeks, pride did not go before a fall. Instead, Nemesis pushed pride off a great height after first tying heavy weights to its ankles. The Athenians once knew this. That is why, after beating back the Persian invasion, they carved the captured Persian stone into a statue of Nemesis and set her up in a temple in the deme of Rhamnos. However, by 416 the Athenians had forgotten this lesson from the past.

Much of the Melian dialogue concerns the question of whether the Melians could expect help from Sparta. The Melians suggested hopefully that the Spartans would come quickly to the aid of a fellow Dorian people in distress. But Athenians knew their Spartans well. They briskly (and correctly) dismissed the only chance Melos might have had. 'When self-interest is at stake, people can act quickly enough. But to take risks for no advantage other than supporting a moral principle requires a certain dynamism. And the Spartans don't have it.'

The Melians ultimately informed the Athenians of their decision. They had been a free people for 700 years and would die that way. Slavery was not an option, and Melos would not yield – even to irresistible force.

The little island state did not go meekly to its doom. At one point her hoplites made a night attack, emerging from behind their walls to capture a part of the Athenian siege lines. Yet the imbalance in power between the two sides could lead to but one result, and Thucydides gives it dispassionately.

> Siege operations were conducted energetically, and forced the Melians to surrender unconditionally to the Athenian army. The Athenians put to death all men of military age. The women and children were sold as slaves. The Athenians took Melos for themselves, later sending out a group of 500 men as colonists.
>
> Thuc. 5.116ff.

This was a relatively minor incident, and certainly the attention Thucydides devotes to it is out of all proportion to the military significance of the event in the war as a whole. Yet what Thucydides tells us is less important than what he shows without saying. Readers see for themselves how far Athens had fallen from the days when the city was the protector of Greek liberty. This is no longer Pericles' shining city on a hill, but a brutal despotism that took almost a grim pleasure in rejecting appeals to justice and fair conduct. Plutarch adds that Alcibiades was the leading proponent of the massacre at Melos and personally helped himself to an enslaved Melian woman who bore his child soon afterwards.[17] For Thucydides, Melos is essential to the story of what happened later in Sicily because at Melos Nemesis opened a file on the arrogance of Alcibiades and on the *hubris* of Athens.

The Melians could not be helped, but Nemesis would see that they were avenged.

Sicily up to 415 BC

Events on the Greek mainland had been watched closely on the island of Sicily. Though hundreds of miles distant from the war, the Greeks in Sicily were descendants of colonists from the cities now doing the fighting. They considered themselves no less Greek for the fact that they shared their island with native peoples (whom they called the Sicels) and the Carthaginians who occupied the south-west of the island. In true Hellenistic style, the Greeks of Sicily occasionally made war on the Sicels, periodically united to fight bitter battles with the Carthaginians, but reserved the greater part of their time and energy for fighting with each other.

In later years, the philosopher Plato was to remark that the Greek colonies of the Mediterranean squatted around the coastline 'like frogs around a pond'.[18] This was certainly true of eastern Sicily, where the Greek presence was most firmly entrenched. The most western cities were Himera on the north coast and Akragas (Agrigento) on the south; both frontier city states constantly on guard against marauders from Carthaginian Motya on Sicily's western tip. Akragas was a second generation colony, as it was founded by the people of Gela, a city that occupied the land to the east of the Himera river, on a site colonized by settlers from the island of Rhodes.

Despite its Dorian antecedents, Akragas was determined to remain neutral in the struggle shaking the Hellenistic world, not least because it was determined to remain part of that world. The risk of Carthaginian conquest made Akragas one of the few Greek cities more concerned about foreign conquest than threats from its neighbours. The same was true of the little city of Camerina, further to the west. This city sympathized with Athens, but had more urgent problems to worry about than a faraway war.

Gela had close ties not only with Akragas, but also with Syracuse, the principal Greek city in Sicily. These ties had been forged in war, for Gela had actually conquered Syracuse in 484 BC. However, it was not in the nature of Greek cities for one to remain subservient to another for long. The Syracusans threw off the tyrant imposed by Gela and set up a democracy. Despite this, the bonds forged over the occupation period remained strong, and many citizens of Gela had relatives in Syracuse.

Syracuse was a huge city, greater in size and wealth than most in mainland Greece. Yet attempts by the Syracusans to extend their power inland or along the coast failed to achieve any permanent success. This is well typified by the small city of Leontini, just 23 miles away. Leontini was highly unusual among Greek cities in Sicily for being situated some 6 miles inland from the sea. The city had been taken from the Sicels by Greeks from northern Sicily and taken from those Greeks by Syracuse in 476. Yet by 417 Leontini was once more independent, and grimly struggling to stay that way with help from Catana, a rival to Syracuse further up the coast within sight of Mount Etna.

On the other side of that rumbling volcano was the town of Naxos, reputed to be the oldest Greek colony in Sicily. This city shared its name with the Cycladean isle of Naxos, but had little else in common with it. The Sicilian Naxos was an Ionian city; in fact, by some reports the founding father was Theocles, an Athenian. Nevertheless, this Naxos was outside the Athenian empire, while the island city state of Naxos was Dorian, and a reluctant conscript to the Athenian cause.

In Sicily there were historic ties between Naxos and Leontini, for Leontini had originally been founded by colonists moving out from the first Greek city on this island. On the north-eastern tip of Sicily was the city of Messene. This colony had originally been called Zancle, but (by one tradition) a later ruler changed its name to that of his homeland city of Messene on the Greek mainland, a city now crushed to helot subservience by the Spartans. The Messenes sometimes traded and sometimes fought with their former colony of Rhegium (modern Reggio di Calabria), one of the oldest Greek settlements on the Italian mainland. Unlike most of Sicily, Messene was allied to Athens.

The Greek cities of Sicily and Italy were considered Magna Graecia – 'greater Greece'. Their peoples were very much sons and daughters of Hellas. They sent competitors to the Olympic games and Pythagoras (inventor of the famous theorem) spent a good part of his life in southern Italy, establishing a reputation for intellectual prowess in the area that later was to draw Plato to Syracuse and in future centuries give birth to the intellectual exuberance of Archimedes.

Yet the Greeks of Sicily were like their mainland compatriots in another way – they could no more co-operate than a herd of cats. Cities fought regular little wars with each other, and within every city political heads of steam built up, with oligarchs resenting democrats and both uniting to hate tyrants. This led to regular explosions of civil strife, and groups of exiles spreading to sympathetic neighbours, there to foment unrest and rebellion back home. In this disunion, the Athenians saw an opportunity.

Sicily at war

As was to be expected of a Greek community, there were as many responses to the outbreak of the Peloponnesian war as there were factions within the various Greek cities. Some states, such as Rhegium in southern Italy, felt strongly pro-Athenian. Others, led by Syracuse – which had been originally founded by settlers from Corinth – backed Sparta and declared war on Athens. The Spartans received cash contributions from some Sicilian cities, and Thucydides mentions that others supplied ships.

Athens had always been aware of the strategic importance of the west. One of the reasons for the outbreak of war was because Corinth resented Athenian attempts to gain control of Corcyra (Corfu), precisely because it was a way station on the voyage to Magna Graecia.

There was also awareness from the Sicilian side. Early in the war, when the Spartan hoplites had been introduced to reality by a solid defeat at Pylos, the Syracusans decided that Messene offered a potential foothold for Athens in Sicily. They launched a brisk invasion of that city state and set up a government more sympathetic to Sparta, while their allies from Locris harassed pro-Athenian Rhegium and stopped that city from sending aid.

In fact, prior to 415, much of the war in the west was fought around Rhegium and Messene. An attempt by the new government of Messene to blockade the harbour of Rhegium failed. This was mainly because Athens sent sixteen ships to support their ally, and the superior seamanship of the Athenian sailors easily offset their enemies' greater numbers.

The Athenian navy turned up in greater strength a bit later and conducted serious operations around Naxos (at one point being interrupted by a minor eruption of Mount Etna), and punished the Locrians for their earlier aggression against Rhegium. This was not an attempt at conquest, but mainly to show wavering allies – particularly Camerina, which was engaged in a minor war with Gela – that Athens could project serious military force that far westward. The ostensible point of the operation was to help Leontini, an Ionian city about to succumb to the Dorian Syracusans, but there was also the intention to interdict corn supplies being sent from Sicily to the Peloponnese.

In fact there was a school of thought that considered the small Athenian force operating around Sicily as a useful training school for operations elsewhere, as neither victory or defeat in this faraway theatre were immediately relevant to the main struggle being fought out in Greece. So there was generally a fleet of some forty Athenian ships operating from Rhegium, giving support to rebellious Sicels, picking on targets of opportunity and generally ensuring that Athenian allies in the area knew that they were not forgotten.

The idea that the Athenians might later take a serious military interest in their island at a later date occurred to some Sicilians. The Athenian fleet operating from Rhegium was not only a constant thorn in the side of the island's pro-Spartan allies, but also an instrument by which the Athenians stayed up-to-date on the Sicilian situation and collected the intelligence information they might need for a future invasion.

A Syracusan called Hermocrates was so convinced of the Athenian threat that he was prepared to stake his political future on it. He was the leading figure at an assembly in Gela where delegates from all the leading cities of Sicily met in 424 to discuss the situation.

As I see it, we are here to discuss Sicily's survival. The island is under threat from Athens, and this alone is a more convincing argument for us to make peace [between ourselves] than anything I could offer. Those few ships they have among us at the moment are waiting for us to make a mistake … or for someone to call in the Athenians, for they are desperately keen to come over here whether we want them or not. By burning our resources in fruitless wars we are laying the foundations for their future empire. Once they see we are exhausted, they will be over here in force …

No one should think they are in particular danger because they are Dorian, or that they are safe because they are Ionian. The Athenians won't do this because they hate the one and love the other but because they want the good things of Sicily, which belong to us all.[19]

The Sicilians saw the sense of this argument, and a sort of peace was patched up across the island. The cities that had formerly hosted the Athenian fleet told its commanders that with the advent of peace in Sicily the Athenian ships were neither needed nor welcome, and invited the Athenians to depart.

There were many who believed that Hermocrates was exaggerating the Athenian menace for his own political advantage, and certainly the Syracusan's political stock soared with the advent of peace. It received a further boost when the news filtered back from Athens that the commanders of the fleet had been punished for not doing more to bring the island under Athenian control. 'By now,' remarks Thucydides, 'their good fortune [in the war to date] had persuaded the Athenians that the difficult and the possible were alike attainable, whether or not the resources deployed were adequate for the job.'[20]

A few years later, with peace looming in Greece, the Athenians sent an ambassador to Magna Graecia. This was something of a fishing expedition intended to check how much support Athens enjoyed in the west. The answer was 'precious little', with the exception of Rhegium and the frontier cities of south-west Sicily. However, the enterprising ambassador went further inland, where he confirmed that the Sicels had little love for the coastal Greek cities, and were thus potentially useful.

This was particularly true of the Elymian people in the far north-west of the island. The Elymians were already loosely allied to the Athenians because their principal city, Egesta, had a mixed population of natives and Ionian Greeks. A sure sign of Hellenization in the city was that it was perpetually at odds with its nearest neighbour, the city of Selinus. By now the peace of Gela was fraying at the edges, and the Egestans were quite willing to get help with their vendetta from wherever they could find it. This was especially so because the Selinites had allied with Syracuse, and the Egestans were on the losing side of the current bout of warfare. It appears from a recently found inscription that Athens already had a treaty with Egesta, but this was probably for mutual defence, and not particularly helpful to the Egestans as we are told they attacked Selinus first.[21]

Nevertheless, exactly as Hermocrates had feared, an Egestan delegation arrived in Athens and asked for support. The delegation's line of argument aimed squarely at Athenian self-interest. The problem, proclaimed the ambassadors, was not Selinus but Syracuse. Syracuse had just taken over much-disputed little Leontini by a particularly blatant act of aggression (and Athens did have a defensive agreement with Leontini). Extrapolating from Leontini's to their own troubles, the Egestans denounced a dark Syracusan plot, by which the cities of Sicily were to be conquered one-by-one, until the whole island was united under Syracuse. Then, Syracuse being Dorian, the combined armies of Sicily would sweep eastward, link up with the Spartans and crush Athens and her empire.

Had they wished, the sophisticated Athenians would have had little trouble pointing out the flaws in this theory. Syracuse might be able to knock over one or two smaller city states, but any serious attempt at empire building would provoke an alliance against the city, with Gela and Catana at the fore. And if, contrary to all expectation, the Sicilian cities did somehow manage to unite, they had the Sicels and the Carthaginians to deal with before attempting an invasion of Athens.

After those obstacles had been overcome, the formidable Athenian navy would have something to say about an invasion fleet setting out from Sicily – and as the Athenians had demonstrated at Rhegium, even a small number of their ships were capable of deadly damage. And should the Sicilians prevail despite all the odds, what would they gain from it? There was no chance of a permanent conquest, and even less chance of holding the Athenian island empire together. Rich as Athens was, it was hard to imagine how plunder could offset the huge costs of such an invasion, and if an invasion of this type were indeed possible, why not start with nearby and even more hostile Carthage?

However, the Athenians wanted to be convinced by the Egestan delegates. For a start, they had commitments to their fellow Ionians in Leontini. Therefore, thoughtful souls in the Athenian assembly, Alcibiades among them, had turned the Syracusan invasion theory on its head and liked the idea from that angle. What if, instead of Sicily invading Athens, the Athenians invaded Sicily? Seen from this perspective, most of the challenges facing the Sicilians disappeared.

An Athenian conquest of Sicily could no more permanently hold down the island than a Sicilian conquest of Athens could keep down Attica. But, especially given Athens' less-than-proud record of keeping surly allies in line, perhaps Sicily could be coerced long enough for the complete resources of the island to be thrown into the war against Sparta? Sicily would gain little if Athens were conquered, so an invasion of Attica had little appeal for the islanders. But Sicily might be used to conquer Sparta, and the idea of a conquered Sparta had huge appeal for the Athenians.

Again, while the Sicilians would have trouble getting an invasion fleet to Greece, Athenian naval dominance meant that an invading fleet would arrive unharassed in Sicily. The Sicels were generally favourable towards the Athenians, and surely a peace could be patched up with the Carthaginians. Though Carthage was a bitter rival of the Sicilian cities, Athenians and Carthaginians had nothing against each other. In short, it was not even remotely possible that Sicily might invade Athens. But could Athens invade Sicily?

Once the delegation from Egesta had put the idea into enterprising Athenian heads, the question that went around the city in the early months of 415 was 'Why not?'

Chapter 3

Travel Plans

The island is a very good one ... The well-watered meadows of soft grass come right down to the grey sea; grapes would do there excellently; there is level land for ploughing, and the soil is deep, promising rich harvests season after season.

Odysseus describes Sicily circa 1000 BC (*Odyssey* 9.120ff.)

For the Athenians of 415, the future looked promising. The city had rebounded strongly and predictably after the initial setback caused by the plague. It was sixteen years since the onset of that catastrophe, and a new generation was preparing to refill the depleted ranks of the Athenian battle-line. In the meantime, the defensive strategy of leaving Attica largely undefended had succeeded, for the Spartans had not even tried to break the walls of Athens.

Since the Spartans had no way of blockading the city, even at the height of the war cargo ships had sailed serenely into the Piraeus, bringing grain and tribute from the city's island empire. Even more perturbing to invading Spartan hoplites had been the sight of Athenian warships sailing out laden with troops and bound for points unknown. Sparta famously had no city walls, so the knowledge that the Athenian army could reach their city before they could had forced the Spartans to keep their pillaging expeditions in Attica short and to the point.

Pylos had been a huge humiliation for Sparta, which even the heroics of Brasidas in Thrace had been unable to avenge. The victory at Mantinea had shown that Sparta remained a dangerous beast if provoked, but currently that beast was sulking in its lair, preoccupied with internal political issues. These mainly revolved around what to do with the hoplites who had disgraced the city by surrendering at Pylos. It was felt that something drastic should be done with them. However many came from the very best families, and punishing Sparta's aristocratic elite was proving problematic.

Overall, Athens felt it had been a pretty good war. They were richer than ever, their enemies were hurt and humiliated, and while they and their friends had been beaten at Mantinea, there still remained the potential for a fruitful alliance with Argos or possibly even Corinth.

Though it was not in the Athenian character to rest on their laurels, even the most blithely bellicose Athenian hesitated before picking another fight with Sparta. The Persian war had for all practical purposes ended in stalemate, so a new outlet was needed for Athenian military enterprise. Sicily seemed to fit all the necessary criteria.

The island was immensely rich and had abundant supplies of grain. It was aligned with the enemies of Athens, but not so closely that there were not several points – Camerina, Messene and Egesta, for example – where a strong bridgehead might be established. At best, Athens might add the whole island to her empire. Even a middling success might bring over at least the Ionian cities. And since the Athenian navy would be standing by to evacuate the entire army should things go disastrously wrong, what was the worst that could happen? Things would go back to as they were at present, but with the new hoplites given some valuable military experience.

Somewhere along this line of argument an Athenian invasion of Sicily went from a provocative idea to a workable theory to the next item on the agenda.

Nicias

The end of the winter once more opened the Mediterranean for navigation. Eurus, the east-blowing wind, brought to Athens a delegation from Egesta bearing promises of sixty talents of silver. Since it cost about a talent a month to keep a warship in business, the Egestans proposed to hire sixty ships for a month. This should be considered a downpayment, for if things went well, the Egesta's temples held a cash reserve that would fund operations well into the summer.

Unsurprisingly, the prospect of being paid for something they were seriously considering doing in any case made up the minds of the Athenian assembly. They voted to send the sixty ships, ostensibly to defend Egesta against Selinus, but also to restore the independence of Leontini, and 'to act as best advanced the interests of Athens'. According to the Sicilian historian Diodorus Siculus (writing in the first century BC) the actual motive was more sinister.

> The generals, meeting in secret conclave with the council, discussed what should be done if Athens did indeed get control of the island. The conclusion was that they would enslave the people of Selinus and the

Syracusans. From the other peoples [of Sicily] they would merely demand an annual tribute to the Athenians.[22]

The sixty ships were fitted out and manned. Only one obstacle remained – one of the fleet's commanders did not want to go. That commander was Nicias, the veteran who had fought through the first phase of the war. He had been involved in early operations on Melos and Pylos, had launched a textbook siege at Megara and Cythera, and afterwards negotiated the peace with Sparta that bore his name.

Nicias, son of Niceratus, was a scion of the old Athenian aristocracy. As a young man he had held command alongside Pericles, and after that leader's death he had led the party opposing the demagogic Cleon. While uniformly successful as a general, Nicias cut a miserable figure as a public speaker. He was easily confused in the assembly and was obviously ill-at-ease at public speaking. He had none of the easy arrogance of Alcibiades, nor that youth's golden tongue.

However, the Athenian people had a soft spot for Nicias, not despite the fact that he was regularly shredded by his opponents in debate, but because of it. He might be a competent general, and numbered among the wealthiest and best-born citizens of Athens, but his hapless performance at public assemblies gave him something of an everyman character that the average Athenian sympathized with.

Furthermore, Nicias had a precise and scrupulous character. Once, having fought and won a battle in Corinthian territory, he collected the Athenian dead and re-embarked his army with the fleet. At this point he realized that he had two of his soldiers unaccounted for, and their bodies must still lie on the battlefield. The enemy had re-occupied the field, so Nicias petitioned them for permission to retrieve these two bodies. By the prevailing laws of war, that side which asked the other for permission to collect its dead was deemed to have lost the battle, but Nicias preferred this shame to that of leaving Athenians unburied.[23]

Another leader of the proposed expedition was to be the steady and experienced Lamachus. The Athenians liked their generalling to be done by a small committee and elected a panel of ten every year for this purpose. They reckoned that the pious and precise Nicias would be the ideal foil for another of the proposed commanders – Alcibiades. While Alcibiades was the man to win over Sicilian cities by charm and diplomacy, the young man had very limited experience of command and an almost limitless capacity for getting into trouble. Also, though Nicias and Alcibiades cordially loathed each other, the two could work well enough together if need be. This had been recently demonstrated when feuding between the pair led to calls for an ostracism.

Ostracism was a peculiarly Athenian institution that worked as a sort of reverse popularity contest. If civil strife appeared to be an issue, Athens would hold an ostracism. Names would be scratched on pot shards (ostraka) and the person who collected the most votes would be exiled for ten years. Since Nicias and Alcibiades were about equally popular, it was touch and go who would be kicked out of the city. The threat was enough to force the two men to collaborate, and between them they engineered the ostracism to take effect on a third character, one Hyperbolus.

This was a popular choice – at least in the eyes of Thucydides, who abandons his usual magisterial calm to venomously remark 'that wretched Hyperbolus was ostracized not because anyone feared his fame or power, but because he was a scumbag and a disgrace to the city'.[24]

Debate

Now, with the matter of the Sicilian expedition already decided, Nicias went to the assembly to try to persuade the population to reconsider. Stripped of rhetoric, the points he made were as follows:

- Point one: Athens had enough enemies right on her doorstep without the need to cross half the Mediterranean just to bring back more. Peace on the Greek mainland was in a pretty shaky condition, and those who wanted war would probably find one in the local theatre in the near future. 'So let the Sicilians have their possessions and quarrels unhindered by us.'
- Point two: Conquering so large and diverse an island as Sicily was difficult to do, but it would be even harder to keep it conquered. If conquering had to be done, there were still bits of Thrace in rebellion against the Athenian empire – surely Athens should look after its own military matters before sub-contracting to sort out those of the Egestans.
- Point three: At the moment Athens had a fearsome reputation, which might not survive any setbacks to the expedition. 'The Greeks in Sicily would fear us most if we never went there at all. Next best would be to go there, make a show of force and then return.' Otherwise, declared Nicias, Athens risked the fate of the Spartans, whom the Athenians had dreaded fighting until they actually had to do so, and now felt confident of beating.
- Point four: If the Athenians must go ahead with this vain, foolish adventure the general they choose should not be a vain, adventurous fool.

There may be someone here who is deliriously happy at being chosen to command despite the fact that he is too young for such responsibility. Someone who urges you to launch this expedition for his own sake, not yours. Perhaps he hopes to defray the ruinous costs of his horse-breeding programme by making a private profit from this venture, in this way putting his city at risk for his own ambition and gain. Remember that those who squander their own fortune will as cheerfully wreak havoc on the public purse. We are talking of something too desperately important to give to a young man to cater for his whims.[25]

Not unnaturally, Alcibiades rose to speak in his own defence, and at that point those who knew of Nicias's record as a debater might as well have left the assembly and started packing for the voyage. Naturally, Alcibiades sought to appear as the voice of sweet reason, and the objections of Nicias as the petulant jealousy of an old man.

'Don't be afraid of me because I am young. Instead, while I still have the energy of youth and Nicias has the reputation of being a lucky general, make the best use that you can of both of us,' Alcibiades urged. Sicily might be large, but its cities were mongrel affairs where no one in the mixed populations would feel he was really fighting for his homeland. 'Everybody spends his time trying to get what he can from the public purse by clever speeches or open extortion. And if things go wrong, such people simply move on and try their luck in another country.'

None of the Greek states in Sicily was properly organized for war, and the number of their hoplites was probably vastly exaggerated, remarked the young orator (brushing aside with a fine rhetorical flourish the fact that the Sicilians had been battling the well-armed and organized Carthaginians for generations). In fact, things would be easier than he was making them out to be, for the native people of the island would happily join in an attack on the Greek cities.

From here Alcibiades moved into full imperialistic mode, telling the assembly that they were 'empire builders, not housekeepers quibbling at numbers'.

The fact is, we are at the point where we have no choice but to plan new conquests if we want to hold on to what we have already. We are a target for others, and we may fall under their power unless we first force them to be under ours. That is the current position – you can't look for a quiet life because our situation is no longer compatible with one. By going abroad we increase our power at home. Even the arrogant types in the Peloponnese will be cowed when they see that we are prepared to take on Sicily. It's quite likely that we can use victory in Sicily to become masters of Greece – and at the worst we will harm the Syracusans, help our allies and do ourselves some good.[26]

To back up his case, Alcibiades wheeled out exiles from Leontini and Egesta who passionately informed their fellow Ionians how they had suffered at the hands of the Dorians. They called on the assembly to remember the ties between their cities and Athens, and to help them in their hour of need. In short, after the intervention of Nicias, the Athenians were no longer eager for action in Sicily. Instead, they positively clamoured for it.

Nicias next revealed a trait in his character that was to have ominous overtones for future developments. He had no idea of when to accept defeat and back away. Instead he plunged on in an attempt to win a battle already lost and so made a bad situation worse. He challenged the weakest point of Alcibiades' argument. The Sicilians were no motley crew of makeshift soldiers, but a well-armed and well-trained force. In loving detail, Nicias ran through the hoplites, archers and javelineers the expedition could expect to face, not to mention heavy artillery in the form of bolt-throwing catapults, and vastly superior cavalry.

Sixty ships were nowhere near enough, proclaimed Nicias passionately. All that sixty ships could do would be to poke the hornet's nest, and then, once the Sicilians were well and truly roused, run back to Athens leaving their allies in the lurch. The only way that the expedition stood a chance was for Athens to commit all the resources it had stored up from the recent peace and all the warriors from the new generation who were now growing into manhood. All this, he announced, would be put at hazard if the Athenians were serious about this madcap adventure. He sat down, confident that he had finally forced the assembly to see things in the light of reason.

The assembly agreed with him. They accepted his case that the Sicilians were better armed and equipped than Alcibiades had asserted they were. They fully agreed that either massive resources should be dedicated to the expedition or it should not go. Then they proceeded to vote the expedition the extra money, men and material that Nicias had claimed that it required. With his usual oratorical skill, Nicias had attempted to stop the Athenians from committing a reasonably strong force to Sicily. He succeeded in getting the assembly to send a massively powerful force instead.

Modern historians have generally considered the launching of the Sicilian expedition as an act of folly. Some believe that the Athenians had no idea of the scale of the venture they were undertaking. While leading Athenians might know better, the average assemblyman simply did not grasp the size of Sicily, the wealth of the island's population and the resources at its disposal. By this argument, had they done so, the Athenians would have hesitated to open a second front against Sicily with so much unfinished business awaiting them at home. After all, the Athenians might have eventually got the better of Sparta, but it had hardly been a painless or easy war – and that war might resume at any moment. If war in the Peloponnese did flare up again, this time Athens would be fighting not only Sparta but another equally powerful opponent at the same time.

As Nicias had pointed out, the Athenians could usefully have deployed their resources in retaking Amphipolis, or extending their dominance across Thrace. They could have concentrated on making a secure alliance with Corinth and Argos, and with those two cities on board seriously pressured Boeotia to make peace and then forced Megara back into their empire. One can imagine Pericles, were he still alive, coming up with a strategy that stripped Sparta of its allies one-by-one until that city was cornered at the bottom of the Peloponnese. Then a judicious attack combined with a helot rebellion might remove the threat to Athens from mainland Greece for a generation, allowing expansion abroad to proceed without hindrance.

But steady, methodical progress was not the Athenian way. Athenians looked for dramatic results from spectacular and daring ventures. In 415 it was the carefree, slightly madcap and highly ambitious Alcibiades who personified the spirit of the people. Like the city he was leading to war, Alcibiades set no limits on what he might achieve and gave little thought to who else might suffer in the course of that achievement.

This mood of confident patriotic pride is neatly captured in the near-contemporary play *The Birds* by the scatological but brilliant playwright Aristophanes, who parodied Athens in a mock-city set up by the birds.

> This most famous of towns, this city in the sky!
> Do you not know how much all men respect you
> How many love this place?
>
> Before you built your city in the air,
> Everyone was crazy about Sparta
> They went around with long hair

> Half-starved and they never washed,
> (Like Socrates – and carrying knobby sticks too.)
>
> These days it's all different
> They're all mad about the birds.
>
> Aristophanes, *The Birds* 1599ff.

In the same play a character who comes up with a clever defence to a sudden assault is told, 'What a grand stroke of warlike strategy! In military matters you're the best – already smarter than Nicias.'[27]

Nicias might be the butt of jokes about his old-maidish character and his inability to win debates, but the Athenians trusted him to win battles. Therefore, since the expedition to Sicily was to take the best Athens could send, there was no question of him getting out of it. Whether he liked the idea or not, Nicias would be one of the joint commanders of the expedition.

Preparations

Though this expedition was to be on an unprecedented scale, the move itself was not unprecedented. A generation previously the Athenians had sent a similar expedition to Egypt in an attempt to wrest at least the northern portion from Persian control. Dozens of minor expeditions had since set out for operations in Thrace and around the islands and coasts of the Aegean. Practise had established a set procedure for such operations.

The ships were partly provided by the state and equipped from the arsenal building in the harbour of the Piraeus. This building – part dry dock, part warehouse and part workshop – now received orders to put ships into commission. The costs of running these new ships would be paid for by 'liturgies'. To be assigned a liturgy was one of the expensive honours top-class Athenian taxpayers bore for the state. Such liturgies might be for the provision of games, or a particular ritual, or as in this case, to kit out and pay for a warship. Those who supplied warships had also the privilege of commanding them and the title of *trierarch*. Most tried to make their ships into floating advertisements for their wealth and prestige, 'spending a fortune on figure-heads and general fittings, with every one keen to make his ship stand out as much for its splendour as its speed'.[28]

However, actually taking the vessel on active military service was optional. Once they had expensively equipped a ship, many liturgists reckoned they had a better chance of keeping it afloat if they handed command to a hired professional.

Other hired professionals on the expedition included mercenary archers from Crete and quite possibly extra rowers for the fleet. The job of rowing ships in ancient Greece was given to free men, usually from the landless class known as *thetes*. However, there are indications that the Athenians were happy to hire mercenary rowers as the need arose, partly to keep a reserve of manpower, but also to prevent such men from powering the triremes of rival states such as Corinth and Sparta. Pay was a drachma per day.

As always, the subject states of the Athenian empire were assessed for their involuntary contribution. Those that paid tribute now sent this to Athens, doubtless with an extra levy to mitigate the costs to the city of her extraordinary effort. Those cities that provided ships and men were given a place (Corcyra) and a time (midsummer) when they were expected to rendezvous with the main fleet from Athens itself. At the same time envoys went to the city states of the Euxine (Black Sea) to negotiate for supplies of corn and other provisions for the expedition.

While Athens paid her citizen soldiers, it did not provide armour or other equipment. This was the individual's responsibility and the type and quality of a man's set of armour and weapons (called a *panoply*) did much to determine his status in the community.

The primary and most distinctive item in the *panoply* was the shield. This shield weighed some 7 kilograms (15½ pounds). It was circular and around 80 centimetres to a metre (31 to 40 inches) in diameter. The facing of the shield was bronze hammered around a wooden frame, and some hoplites liked to affix a leather skirt to the bottom of the shield to absorb missile strikes. In battle, the shield partly protected the bearer and partly the man to his left. The weight of the shield was generally borne by a handle set into the side of the back with a strap in the middle for the forearm, but the sharp backward curve of the rim made it possible to hook a shoulder underneath and support the shield in that way as well.

The Spartans famously decorated their shields with the inverted V (*lambda*) of their land of Lacadaemonia, but the individualistic Athenians preferred a variety of motifs, with gorgons and fighting cocks among the favourites. After the shield, the next-best method of terrifying the enemy with one's good taste in armour was the helmet. These tended toward high-crested affairs that completely covered the head and face apart from the eyes and mouth. This 'Corinthian' style was almost universally popular, partly because the cheek guards gripped the head, allowing the helmet to be worn thrust back when the wearer was not in active combat. Other styles such as the Illyrian and Thracian were more open, and these were generally favoured by lighter troops, for whom good vision was more important.

The hoplite's main offensive weapon was his spear. This was around two metres long, and was designed not to be thrown, but to be used for stabbing overhand while in a formed battle line.

Helmet, shield and spear made up the minimum that a citizen could posses and still call himself a hoplite. However, a well-dressed warrior would want body armour and a sword to complete the set. The body armour was a cuirass protecting the torso, and could be stiffened linen, boiled leather or bronze plate according to taste. Greaves protected the legs, and also provided a rest against which a shield could be propped to give the shield-bearing arm some relief. Again, body armour decoration reflected the wearer's personal style.

Swords played little part in a standard infantry battle, but were extremely useful for more informal types of military action and could make the difference between life or death once a battle line had broken. Swords varied as greatly as the tastes of the owner. Some liked a blade slightly curved in the Thracian style, which made the weapon a formidable slashing tool of the 'kukri' type still favoured by the Gurkha today. Others opted for a straight blade, which allowed stabbing as well, but everyone preferred kit that had been tried in battle, and preferably by a few generations of ancestors.

This was not only because there was considerable prestige in fighting in the same *panoply* as one's father had done (the state would replace for a son the *panoply* of a father lost in battle), but for practical reasons as well. The Greeks knew that iron became steel through the use of charcoal in the smelting process, but the exact process was a mystery. Carbonizing steel was a very hit-and-miss process. The quality of any given item might vary from too much carbon, which made steel brittle and likely to shatter, to too little, which made it bendy. Therefore items that had been extensively field-tested were preferred to weaponry fresh from the forge.

Nevertheless, the small workshops of the Piraeus were probably frantically busy in the weeks leading up to the launching of the expedition as equipment was patched and serviced, sharpened and gilded. This was to be the mightiest force the city had ever dispatched and every hoplite was determined to outshine his neighbour with the splendour of his *panoply*. There was no chance of outshining Alcibiades. He had some of the planks of his ship cut away so that his bed was not on the deck, but hanging on a sort of hammock. His shield, richly gilded, bore none of the standard Athenian emblems, but a cupid wielding a thunderbolt. This ostentation combined with flouting of tradition caused further unease among the Athenians and reminded them of the veiled warning Aristophanes had slipped into one of his plays.

> Our city should not rear lions – that's true;
> But treat them like lions if you do.[29]

The silence of the herms

As the expedition prepared to embark, a bizarre and unsettling incident occurred, which has thereafter been one of the enduring mysteries of antiquity. The details of the case are as follows.

All Greek cities, but Athens in particular, had an abundance of herms. Herms were tapering pillars of stone or bronze with a bust on the top. The Athenians (naturally) claimed credit for developing this form of sculpture, which had developed from the piles of stone once used to mark road junctions.

As the name suggests, most herms were topped by a bust of Hermes, the god of boundaries. Such herms could be found in the Agora, outside private houses, at the entrance to sanctuaries and at crossroads. Somewhat disconcertingly for those unused to the sculptural genre, apart from head and shoulders at the top, the stone pillar generally sported a set of male genitalia at the appropriate height on the otherwise featureless column (that is, if the god were indeed Hermes or another male deity – female herms such as Aphrodite were allowed their modesty). For Athenians, herms were everyday street furniture, routinely extending their blessings and protection to the city, and generally ignored (in a reverential way) during the bustle of daily life. They were, as Thucydides says, 'a national institution'.

Then in one night nearly all the herms of Athens were mutilated. The shocked citizens awoke the next morning to find that their herms had been hacked about, their faces cut and chipped and other outstanding features mutilated. This was an act of vandalism and desecration wrapped in a single sacrilegious package. Given the number of herms and the extent of the damage, it was clear that someone had expended a considerable amount of energy and at least some planning on perpetrating the outrage. But who had done it and why?

It did not take long for the outraged Athenians to generate a slew of conspiracy theories. Some felt it had been done by Corinthian agents, or even Syracusans who wanted to discourage the Athenian fleet. But such ideas had few followers. The general feeling was that it was a plot to overthrow the city's democracy. How government by the people was to be overthrown by nocturnal attacks on statuary was currently unclear. However, this was doubtless but the first move in a sinister and deep-laid plot. This theory proved to be popular and large amounts of money were offered by the authorities for any person, citizen, subject or slave who could shed light on exactly how the conspiracy was supposed to unfold.

A few slaves came tentatively forward. They had no specific information about this particular outrage, but had noted that on occasion young aristocrats under the influence of alcohol had been known to attack herms as an outlet for their high spirits. It was not uncommon for such young men to get together for an evening symposium. Such symposiums were not, as in today's world, gatherings of high-minded individuals for the discussion of serious topics. Certainly some individuals (i.e. Socrates) might hijack the proceedings and turn a symposium into a colloquium, but the purpose of an Athenian symposium is clear from the name, which means 'drinking together'.

For every symposium that discussed the meaning of the universe there were a dozen that featured heavy drinking, party games and a general orgy involving those guests still upright and female entertainers laid on for the occasion. It was not unusual for the quiet of the city night to be shattered by a bawdy gaggle of revellers staggering from one symposium to join friends at another. So theory two, about one such group having taken it into their addled heads to attack a herm and the idea having caught on in a form of group madness, hardened.

The attack on the herms was not just an outrage and not just sacrilege. It was also an attack on the city's propriety, and a terrible omen. So the probable suspect was young, rash, aristocratic and with a taste for being outrageous. And since the attack needed a reasonably hard-working team to pull it off, the aforesaid outrageous young man had to be the leader of a like-minded group. The Athenians had never developed psychological profiling into a science, but they had a pretty good idea of where to start. Suddenly, everyone was looking at Alcibiades.

Alcibiades was forced to defend himself in the assembly. Like the rest of the city, he had no doubt that eventually the responsibility for the attack on the herms would be laid at his door, and he wanted to get it over with. The expedition was on the verge of sailing, and the last thing it needed was one of its commanders under suspicion of treason and sacrilege. So let the charges be laid, and Alcibiades would rebut them in court. There was a very good chance that he would be acquitted. After all, there was no direct or even circumstantial evidence that implicated Alcibiades. That this was just the sort of thing he would do was good enough for rumour, but not enough to build a case upon.

The personal charm of Alcibiades had played a large part in persuading almost a thousand volunteers from Mantinea and Argos to join in the expedition. It was immediately clear that some of these would leave if Alcibiades was not to lead them, and furthermore, the Athenian soldiers of the expedition also supported him strongly. The Athenian people were aware of all this, and in the absence of hard evidence against him, this might be enough to sway a jury.

Alcibiades was well aware that out of sight is out of mind. He argued passionately that it was preposterous for a commander to go to war with such charges hanging over him. Let the Athenians try him and condemn him, or let him to go war with the matter settled, but settled it should be one way or the other.

But Alcibiades had angered and humiliated the top men in Athens once too often. These men knew that it were possible for the charges to be stayed until Alcibiades had been away for a week or two, then a whispering campaign could turn public opinion against him. It was important for Alcibiades' political future that a trial should take place at once, and for that very reason his many opponents voted to delay matters pending further investigation.

The expedition would sail with a shadow over the man who was its driving force. And if the mutilation of the herms were not inauspicious enough, the new moon signified the start of the feast of Adonis. As was traditional, the city was decked with images of the dead and women re-enacted the funerals of the departed, so that the environs resounded with their mournful dirges. Overall, the preparations for launch day could have gone better.

Launch day

Nevertheless, when the time came for the expedition to actually set out, it did so in style. Thucydides takes up the tale as he probably heard it himself from eyewitnesses.

At dawn those going on the expedition went down to the Piraeus and boarded the ships. Everyone else in Athens, be they citizen or foreigner, went down with them. Everybody had someone to bid farewell to – a friend, a relative or a son. The men were beginning a voyage that would take them far from their homeland, so this was a moment full of hope and dread. There was the thought of potential conquests for the city, and the knowledge that some now leaving would never return, yet they drew strength from the huge military force laid out before them.

The foreigners in the crowd were there simply there to wonder at the incredible ambition of it all, and to admire the show. It was a fine show indeed, the most splendid and richly equipped force that had ever set sail from a Greek city …

Apart from fifty ships from Chios and Lesbos, there were many ships from other allies as well, and 100 ships of Athens, sixty warships and forty transports carrying 4,000 Athenian hoplites, and 300 cavalry.

Eventually the ships were manned and all that was needed for the voyage had been loaded. A trumpet blast commanded all to silence, and the customary prayers of those putting out to sea were said. This was not done individually by each ship, but by the entire fleet speaking as one, following the words of a herald. Libations were poured into bowls, and from there officers and soldiers made their offerings with gold and silver cups. Then with the paean sung, and the last libation poured, the ships turned out to sea, first sailing in line, and then racing each other out towards [the island of] Aegina.[30]

Chapter 4

The Athenians are Coming!

Shame on the lot of you! At Olympia and Delphi, and dozens more places than I can say, you share the same cup before the same altars as all the other Greeks, yet you go pillaging Greek cities, and stain Greek lands with the blood of their sons.

Aristophanes, *Lysistrata* l.1310

The debate

Athenian people had been right to discount the theory that Syracusans had plotted to mutilate the herms by way of discouraging the expedition against them. News travelled slowly around the ancient Mediterranean, and most Sicilians were convinced that talk of an Athenian invasion force was bluster, or at least exaggerated. Far from trying to convince the Athenians not to attack them, most Syracusans did not think that the Athenians were coming at all.

Certainly it was common knowledge that Athens was fitting out a fleet, but the size of that fleet was as much a topic for debate as the intentions of its commanders. There was also a strong suspicion among Syracusan democrats that talk of an Athenian invasion was being whipped up so that their citizens would give up their hard-won rights and once again put themselves into the power of aristocratic generals. A Syracusan called Athenagoras spoke for the doubters at a public meeting.

I'm not surprised by the impudence of those people who spread this kind of news and try to terrify you with it, but I'm astonished by their stupidity. Do they seriously think that we cannot see what they are trying to do?

These reports have not arrived in the city in the normal course of events. They've been made up by those same people (yes, I'm looking at you, Hermocrates) who are constantly crying wolf on this issue.

Let's consider the Athenians. A clever people and experienced at warfare. Now, what are they likely to do? Would they leave the Peloponnese unsettled, with a major war unfinished, just to start another war just as serious over here? If you ask me, the Athenians are simply glad that we have not used the number and strength of our cities to go on the offensive against them.

Sicily is not Sparta, and if the Athenians did come, Syracuse is better equipped and stronger, even if this supposed invasion force is twice as big as it is made out to be. Where are their cavalrymen going to get their horses from? The Egestans cannot supply them all, and no one else will. And how many hoplites can they bring if they have to come by sea? Fewer than we have here already, I'll tell you. It's hard enough to get any kind of fleet all the way here, even if they travel light. But if they are planning going to war with a full-sized city such as ours, they would have to carry a lot.

Look, even if they brought a city the size of Syracuse and built it right next to us, they would still hardly have a chance – and that's before we consider that they will have the whole of the rest of Sicily against them, as it would be. Realistically, though, they'd manage a tent city at best, equipped with the bare necessities and our cavalry making sure they have not the slightest chance of getting any more. But that's if they can even establish a bridgehead, and taking everything into account, I don't think they'd do even that.

The Athenians know this, and far from looking to expand their empire, I'm sure that they know they're going to have enough trouble hanging on to what they've got already.

So what we have here are people making up stories that are not true and never will be true. I've seen people like this before. In fact I see them all the time. When they can't do what they want, they make up scare stories like this, or even more diabolical stuff, just to panic the crowd into handing over the government to them. They keep trying, and I'm really worried that one day they are going to get away with it ...

So here's what I ask myself about these people. What are you young men really after? Do you want positions of power right now? That's against the law, because the law is not against competent officials but was specifically enacted with people like you in mind. Or can you just not bear living by the same rules as everyone else? [...] You are fools – the stupidest of all Greeks, if you don't see that what you want is evil, and if you are not fools and actually do see this and want to go ahead anyway, then you are criminals ... So give up spreading these rumours. We know what your game is, and we won't put up with it.

The most dogged of the stormy petrels predicting war was Hermocrates, the same aristocrat who had persuaded the people of Sicily to stop the inter-city wars that had previously given the Athenians an excuse to interfere in the affairs of the island. Hermocrates' political stock had risen with the subsequent peace, and now it worked against him. People like Athenagoras insisted that the Athenian Menace was simply a vehicle designed to carry the flag of Hermocrates' ambitions. Yet Hermocrates was sure that the threat was real.

> I know that what I'm telling you sounds incredible. It's the truth, but when a person says something like this, or comes up with news that is so hard to believe, he not only can't convince people, they think he is an idiot for telling them. But I know what I know and I am sure about it. I will not be intimidated, and I will not pipe down when my city is in danger. I know what I am talking about better than some others. (Yes, Athenagoras, I'm looking at you.)
>
> However surprising it might seem, the Athenians are coming for you with a very large force … you have to be clear in your minds that they will be here soon. Start making plans how we can use our resources to confront them. Take this invasion lightly, and it will take you off guard. Disbelieve it, and you turn your back on everything that matters.

Hermocrates went on to reassure his audience that he was sure that any Athenian invasion force was doomed to failure – but only if the people of Syracuse heeded his advice and took the necessary measures to defend themselves.

> We need to reach out to the Sicels. If we have treaties of friendship or alliances, we need to make sure that these are dependable, and if we don't have them we need to make them. We need to contact the other Greek cities in Sicily, and point out that this is not a threat to Syracuse, but a threat to us all. We need to send messengers to the Greek cities in Italy, and make allies there, and try to make sure that no one there welcomes the Athenians.
>
> And yes, we should also reach out to the Carthaginians. They won't be surprised by this news. They are already apprehensive that one day Athens would one day mount an attack against them. So they will probably realize that if they stand back when we are attacked they'll soon be in trouble themselves. Therefore they might well help us, even if they

will not publicly admit the fact. And they can help us more than any state could, because they have large reserves of gold and silver, and, as with anything else, such resources allow a war to be conducted more easily.

Let's ask Sparta, let's ask Corinth, not just for help over here, but to re-start the war back in Greece.

Our best course of action is one that is going to be hard for you stick-in-the-muds to grasp. I doubt that you will get the idea, but here it is. Get all the cities of Sicily to combine their efforts. Then launch every ship we have, loaded with two months' worth of supplies and sail for the promontory of Iapygia, with the idea of taking on the Athenians before they even reach Tarentum. We need to show them that before they even think of fighting for Sicily they have to fight their way across the Ionian Sea. This will make them think twice. They'll realize that we are on guard, and once we've got Tarentum to receive us, we've got a friendly base behind us, and they have nothing but the empty sea to fall back on. They'll have just crossed that sea, and because of the length of the voyage they'll have lost their order and be coming at us in dribs and drabs.

Even if they do manage to lighten their warships and put them into battle mode, we can either attack them if we see that they are tired out from rowing for so long, or fall back on Tarentum. The Athenians will be short of rations, so they'll have to split their fleet if they want to blockade us – and the part of the fleet that sails on will not know whether or not any cities will welcome them. Personally, I think that once they hear that the cities of Sicily have a fleet waiting for them, they won't even leave Corcyra. They'll fritter away the summer in discussions, and send out scouts to find out our position and numbers, and winter will be on them before they know it.

Alternatively, our move might take them so much by surprise that they will give up the expedition altogether. I've been told that their most experienced general's heart is not in the job. He will jump at any excuse to turn back, such as an indication from us that we are serious ...

It's this daring action that I'm most eager that you should take. But if you won't, then at least make all the other preparations for war. Make them as quickly as possible. Contempt for an attacker is best shown by the bravery with which one meets the attack, but right now, the safest steps we can take are those driven by fear. We have to act as though we are aware of the danger.

The Athenians are coming, the Athenians are already on their way ... the Athenians are very nearly here!

Preparations

Once the Syracusan assembly had weighed up the opposing arguments, the general feeling was that Hermocrates had blown matters up out of all proportion. Nevertheless, there could be little harm in seeing if the cities of Sicily were sufficiently spooked by the prospect of an Athenian invasion to unite under the leadership of Syracuse. Likewise, preparing war material, horses and weaponry may or may not be necessary, but the exercise had few disadvantages.

In fact, one suspects a certain degree of *Realpolitik* in the eventual decision. Many Syracusans felt that Hermocrates and his party were using the threat of an Athenian invasion to panic the people into handing themselves over to aristocratic leadership. This did not stop the city as a whole from investigating whether the threat of an Athenian invasion might not panic the cities of Sicily into handing themselves over to Syracusan leadership. And should the threatened invasion fail to materialize, the Syracusans would have an army right on hand to sternly rebuke any who had rebutted their offer of friendship. So, overall, the city did not expect to be attacked, but there were advantages to acting as though it might be.

The idea of a joint Sicilian fleet to throw back the invasion was rejected out of hand, as Hermocrates had predicted it would be, and given the prowess of the Athenian fleet probably should have been. Both to contemporaries and later historians the idea was at best risky and at worse suicidal.

Nor did any Sicilian cities throw themselves whole-heartedly behind the Syracusan cause. However, there was a wary recognition that the Syracusans might have a point. News that the Athenians were preparing a large fleet had got around, and so had news of the attack on Melos. We are told nothing of preparations in Sicily or Italy, but it seems reasonable to believe that across the region weapons were sharpened, city walls strengthened and the citizen muster-rolls checked.

At that same moment, across the sea in southern Italy, Nicias was arguing yet again for chucking in the whole expedition. The Athenians had just discovered that the Egestans had tricked them. The city was desperate for Athenian aid, but despite their promises, they could not afford to pay for it. Their vast financial resources with which they had offered to hire the Athenian fleet turned out to be a sham. The treasure that Athenian envoys had seen piled up in the temples in apparently artless confusion had in fact been carefully arranged, with bulky items such as cups and bowls used to take up more space than solid bars of bullion would do.

And many of these cups and bowls were borrowed, both from private citizens of Egesta and whatever wealthy Egestans had been able to scrounge from their contacts in nearby cities. Once the ambassadors had seen the temple gold, each was entertained for the evening by a different Egestan aristocrat. The envoys were unaware both that they now used the same cups and bowls at dinner that had been in the temple earlier, and that dinners were rushed through or delayed so that the same cups and bowls could be used at meal after meal.

As a result of this deception the Athenian ambassadors had returned home with stories of the jaw-dropping wealth of the Egestans. And since Egesta was a relatively poor and out-of-the way city to the north-west of Sicily, the Athenians had extrapolated from the apparently great wealth of Egesta to assume that almost limitless supplies of booty and tribute could be extracted from the larger and more prosperous cities on the eastern coast.

Then, with the Athenian forces preparing to climb into this supposed cornucopia, the ships sent to Egesta to collect the promised monthly stipend returned with the information that a paltry thirty talents in bullion were available. The unfortunate bearer of the news also carried the admission that the wages – half the amount promised for each month – would have to constitute the Athenians' pay for the entire war. That was everything the Egestans had.

The discovery that the Egestans were poor affected more than the payment arrangements for the fleet. It also cast into doubt the *raison d'être* of the entire expedition. The whole point of conquering Sicily was to put the island's abundant resources to use against the rest of the Greek mainland cities. Now, if Egesta were anything to go by, those resources were just not that abundant. For Nicias, this was reason enough to turn around and go home. If they did not do that, he argued, that the next best thing was to do exactly as the Egestans had contracted them for, and to wage thirty talents worth of war on the rival city of Selinus. Then, with the money used up, the fleet should stage an imposing sail-by of the cities on the Sicilian coast, and then return no better and no worse off than they had been before they set out.

In fact, of the expedition's three joint commanders, Nicias was the least surprised and disappointed by the news from Egesta, because his natural pessimism had led him to assume the worst anyway. However, since then Nicias had found further reasons for gloom. The crossing to Italy had gone smoothly, but the Italian Greeks were less than pleased to see the Athenian fleet. Alcibiades had reckoned that his smooth tongue combined with the implicit threat of the expeditionary force would win co-operation along their route, if not actual friends. Instead, city after city had shut its gates against them. Usually the arrival of such a force would have been a godsend for the small traders of a city, since even as well-equipped a force as the Athenians had soldiers who needed to shop for food and other materials. However, even those cities that did reluctantly set up markets for the fleet would not let the men within their walls. Tarentum, the only colony founded by Sparta, stayed true to the mother city and adamantly refused to have anything to do with the Athenians. Nor did the Locrians offer even a market, which surprised no one, since the Athenians had handled them roughly in their earlier disputes with Rhegium.

It was at Rhegium that the Athenian fleet finally made its temporary base. Even Rhegium, despite having accepted Athenian help in its struggles with Locris, was no more than neutral. The city council refused to join in the 'liberation' of Leontini, even though the two cities shared a common ancestry. So it was under these circumstances that Nicias suggested that if they were going to get neither money nor even a warm welcome from the western Greeks, the Athenians might as well go home.

However, if Nicias had few illusions about what awaited the fleet in Sicily, the other two commanders had even fewer illusions about what would happen if they returned to Athens after a mission that had promised so much and delivered so little. Nicias had the least to concern himself about on this score. He was on record as having claimed from the start that the expedition was a bad idea, and was wealthy enough to face a large fine or even exile with some equanimity.

On the other hand, either a fine or exile would be the ruin of Lamachus. The man was a solid and competent soldier, but so poor that he had to charge the Athenian state for his shoes and cloak while he was on campaign. Aristophanes affectionately mocked his fiery nature in *The Acharnians*, a play in which one character calls for help from: 'Lamachus, whose glance flashes lightning, whose plumed helmet petrifies his enemies, help! Lamachus, my friend, the hero of my tribe!'

This blunt soldier decided that under the circumstances the best approach would be to stop beating about the bush and admit what everyone already knew. The expedition was not aimed at petty Silenus and its squabble with Egesta. It was there to conquer Sicily, and might as well start with Syracuse.

Lamachus pointed out that at the moment many Syracusans still thought that the invasion was a hoax and even those half-convinced had not yet readied their defences. Attack now, he said, before those outside the city walls realized their peril and brought their property and themselves within the city walls. With prisoners and plunder, not to mention the terror that their sudden arrival would cause, the invaders would be off to a good start. Also, by putting Syracuse immediately under siege, the Athenians would greatly increase the number of cities that either came over to Athens, or at least decided to stay neutral.

Alcibiades had yet another opinion. The Athenians should work slowly up to the assault on Syracuse, first building a coalition of the willing and then adding to it with the mixture of diplomacy and coercion that had built the city's island empire in the Aegean. The Sicels should be persuaded to rise against the Syracusans. Above all, Messene should be charmed or forced into providing a harbour for the fleet. That city's position in north-east Sicily made it a natural forward base for any force with supply lines stretching back to Greece. In Alcibiades' own words, 'Messene is the gateway to Sicily.' With Messene secure and a clear knowledge of who was for them and against them, the generals could decide whether to besiege Syracuse or at least force that city to terms. To Alcibiades, even a strong showing that ended in failure would be better than not having tried at all. As one who planned a long career at the forefront of Athenian politics, the worst thing the expedition could do would be return to Athens with nothing to show for it.

The committee of three generals was deadlocked by three opposing opinions. The situation might have grimly amused Lamachus had he recalled that in *The Archanians* a few years before Aristophanes had the character playing him declaim to the audience: 'Ah, the Generals! They are numerous, but not good for much.'

The coalition that wasn't

In the end it came down to which general was going to abandon his plan and vote with one of the others. All three knew that the tie-breaker was going to be Lamachus. With the possible exception of Demosthenes, the man was the best soldier in Athens, but he lacked the political clout of either Alcibiades or Nicias. He stood no chance against the pair combined and he knew it. So he abandoned his own – militarily sound – idea and aligned himself with Alcibiades on the basis that at least the latter's plan was closer to his own intentions than the plan of Nicias.

At this point it appears that command of the expedition split neatly between the three commanders, with each taking the role that played to his strengths. Alcibiades took charge of executing the plan he had devised and set about winning allies through diplomacy. The precise and detail-orientated

Nicias looked after the housekeeping, logistics and day-to-day administration of the fleet, and Lamachus handled what little fighting there was. Two parts of this three-part system worked. The expedition ran smoothly, and it fought competently. Diplomatically, it got nowhere.

Alcibiades started work by taking his own gloriously gilded ship to Messene. There he found that the gateway to Sicily was politely but firmly closed against him. All that charm and threats could produce were an offer to give a market, and that well outside the city walls. Frustrated, Alcibiades returned to Rhegium, where he decided that his error had lain in being too subtle with his threats. Future diplomatic missions would involve not just the golden trireme of Alcibiades, but the entire Athenian fleet of warships – an implicit stick parked just offshore to balance the blandishments that Alcibiades offered as carrots ashore.

The whole-fleet approach was sufficient persuasion for the people of Naxos. They were pro-Athenian in the first place, and the size of the Athenian fleet easily brought over the doubters. Alcibiades had achieved his first goal – a friendly base in Sicily itself. In the event, though, Naxos proved to be the exception rather than a momentum changer. Catana was split between pro-Athenian democrats and pro-Syracuse oligarchs, and at the moment the oligarchs had the upper hand. After a quick investigation proved that further investment of time and effort would be needed to win over the city, the Athenians moved down the coast.

If the Syracusans still had any doubt of the reality of the Athenian invasion force, the next stop of the fleet removed any of this, for ten Athenian ships sailed into the Great Harbour of Syracuse itself. Syracuse had two harbours, and the Athenians were later to become intimately familiar with both. These harbours, the Little and the Great, lay to the north and south respectively of a headland called Ortygia. Ortygia had originally been an island just off the mainland. Islands such as this, very close to but not part of the mainland, were preferred settlement sites for Greek colonists. The islands offered access to the area to be colonized while remaining secure from the outraged natives who currently occupied that land. As generally happened, with increasing prosperity the original colony had later expanded on to the mainland, and what had originally been a causeway linking the old and new cities was now a stretch of land 100 yards across.

The whole area was well-fortified, and the size and extent of these walls was undoubtedly another feature of the city in which the Athenian visitors took a keen interest. The fleet waited in line outside the harbour, ready to promptly deal with any trouble that might follow if their ten ships had to leave hastily. The Athenian ships were deliberately poking a potential hornet's nest. Part of their brief was to see what sort of fleet the Syracusans had, if it was ready for war and if so, whether it was prepared to fight. If the latter was correct, it was assumed that the Syracusans would not tolerate such a blatant intrusion into their harbour. In the event, for reasons now unknown, the Syracusan warships failed to make an appearance.

The second reason for the ships sailing into the harbour was to announce their presence to the Syracusans lining the city walls and for heralds on the ships to proclaim the Athenian *causus belli* – the intention to force Syracuse to restore the freedom of the city of Leontini. To this purpose the herald also announced that any citizens of Leontini currently within the walls of Syracuse would be well-advised to remove themselves from the area as soon as possible.

Thereafter, since the Syracusan ships showed no inclination to come out and play, the Athenians busied themselves with ostentatiously and very pointedly taking notes of the city's fortifications, potential weak spots and suitable landing sites for the army. Then the expedition sailed off to the north, leaving the Syracusans with a veritable banquet of food for thought.

The Athenian fleet now returned to Catana, where Alcibiades planned to overcome his earlier rebuff. Catana was torn between a pro-Athenian populace and a pro-Syracuse aristocracy, with the latter holding power. Alcibiades now intended to use Athenian might to tip the balance of power in Catana towards the pro-Athenian democrats. Arriving at the city, Alcibiades obtained permission to address the popular assembly. While his rhetoric was quite possibly powerful, it proved nowhere near as persuasive as the Athenian sailors, who took advantage of the distraction of the assembly meeting to break down a minor gate in the city walls. Gradually, the people of Catana listening to Alcibiades became aware that the rest of the city was filling up with armed Athenians.

The democrats rapidly realized that their allies could now give them control of the city even as the oligarchs realized that they had lost it. The latter did not even try to dispute what was in effect an Athenian-sponsored bloodless *coup d'état*. They swiftly gathered their families and moveable possessions and quit the city, leaving Alcibiades with a second diplomatic triumph and a secure base not far from Syracuse.

Momentum finally seemed to be building. Tidings came that the small, pro-Athenian city of Camerina was prepared to commit to the Athenian side. This was great news, because just as Catana was north of Sicily, Camerina was south-west. Occupation of both cities would allow the Athenians to bracket their main enemy with hostile bases. The Syracusan navy was also reported to have come out of its funk and be preparing to offer battle, so after ordering the transports at Rhegium to bring the army over to Catana, Alcibiades ordered the warships south. If all went well, he would arrive at Camerina bearing news that the Syracusan fleet had been sunk behind him – information sufficient to overwhelm the reservations of the last doubters. In short, the diplomatic solution was beginning to work after all.

It would be a long time before Alcibiades could feel so hopeful again.

The trip south was a waste of time. The war-hardened Athenian sailors had been looking forward to teaching their Syracusan counterparts a thing or two about naval warfare, but either the Syracusans had realized they were outmatched or the rumour that they were planning to put to sea had been false in the first place. Either way, the fleet encountered no Syracusan ships, and Alcibiades had no victory to present to the Camerinans. This was unfortunate, because again, as with the Syracusan navy, either the rumours were false, or second thoughts had followed the first report. Camerina was now determined to remain neutral.

The Athenians were informed that, as stipulated in the treaty that Hermocrates had hammered out six years ago at Gela, they would allow only one Athenian ship into their harbour. The city obdurately refused to be won over by Athenian arguments, and eventually the fleet had to sail north once more. Possibly in order to have something to show for his wasted trip, Alcibiades allowed his sailors to raid Syracusan territory on the way home. This formally opened hostilities with Syracuse and incidentally confirmed the opinion of Lamachus that a sudden descent on the city might have been productive. The Athenians captured a number of stragglers making their way into Syracuse now that it had been proven beyond a doubt that the Athenians had arrived. Had the expedition arrived unexpectedly and set up shop a few weeks earlier, when the Syracusans dismissed reports of the Athenian expedition as scaremongering, the number of prisoners and amount of plunder would have been immeasurably greater.

As it was the fleet gathered up its meagre booty and returned to Catana. Here a bad few days for Alcibiades suddenly got much worse. The *Salamina* had arrived while Alcibiades was away. This ship was one of two state messenger ships of the Athenian people. It was used for missions of great importance and urgency. The ship's current task was to take Alcibiades on board and bring him back to Athens, there to face charges of treason and sacrilege.

Meanwhile, back in Athens …

Once they had dispatched the city's finest on their mission to conquer first Sicily and then the rest of the known world, the Athenian people did not sit back to confidently await results. Instead they began neurotically to pick over the mutilation of the herms and whatever sinister meaning lay behind it. The obvious first step was to find the mutilators. Neighbour looked at neighbour with angry suspicion and uncertainty, and the idea that it was all some sort of plot to overthrow the democracy took ever firmer root in the popular imagination.

Since the obvious beneficiaries of the overthrow of democracy were the aristocrats, a number of aristocrats were seized on precautionary grounds and imprisoned. At the centre of the storm was an aristocratic drinking club headed by one Andocides. An informer called Teucer had given evidence against this group, and though those concerned were seized, the search for culprits went on. Then one Diomedes claimed he could identify Euphiletus as the perpetrator of the deed as he had seen the faces of the villains by moonlight as they went about their nefarious act. This puzzled the more rational type of Athenian, since the Athenians set their calendar by the phases of the moon, and it was common knowledge that the moon had barely been a sliver in the sky when the crime was carried out. Common knowledge was evidently more common than common sense, since the general populace were by now too desperate for a scapegoat to let facts stand in their way.

Nor did it worry people that either Teucer or Diomedes had to be lying and that at least one set of innocent aristos had been arrested. Then, just to ratchet the tension up a bit further, Spartan troops were reported advancing northwards, and the Thebans were arming. A logical mind might have assumed that the Spartans had in mind intimidating Argos or Corinth and Thebes was preparing to take whatever advantage it could from the situation. This explanation did not satisfy the fevered imagination of the Athenians, who were convinced that this was the next step of whatever plan had begun with the mutilation of the herms.

With every aristocrat in prison facing either lynching or a kangaroo court, the prisoners put pressure on one – any one – of their number to confess. In the end Andocides stepped forward with a confession. He named himself and his cronies as the guilty parties, taking care to implicate mostly those who had decided to get out of Athens while the going was good. He also informed the populace that the group had no particular motive. A drunken game had simply got well out of hand.

The Athenian people were delighted with having got to the bottom of the matter and with the whole business having turned out to be so harmless (the Spartans had since gone home without doing anything and the Thebans had stood down). Consequently, they freed the informant and everyone he had not named. The others were evidently guilty of sacrilege and were charged and condemned according to proper judicial process. Thucydides comments caustically, 'It was impossible to say whether or not the condemned deserved their punishment, but it was quite clear that as things were, the city settled down and so everyone else benefited greatly.'

The mutilation of the herms being now concluded to general satisfaction, this left certain Athenian politicians with the problem that no one had pinned anything on Alcibiades. Certainly he had been a prime suspect, and some members of his family had been roughly handled by their accusers, but the informant had rather annoyingly neglected to include Alcibiades among the nocturnal statue smashers. Another means would have to be found to bring Alcibiades down, and preferably while the populace were still enjoying the taste of judicial lynching.

It has been credibly suggested that among those working for the downfall of Alcibiades were those aristocrats arrested following the now-discredited testimony of Diomedes. These men believed that Diomedes had been put up to presenting his story to the authorities either by Alcibiades or his friends in order to deflect suspicion from themselves. As might be expected of men who had escaped death by the skin of their teeth, they were understandably bitter about this. Those accused by Diocledes included members of the powerful Alcmaeoenid clan and, probably not co-incidentally, Andocides, who had got them off by backing Teucer's story about himself, the informer who had got them off by backing Teucer's story, came from a family closely allied with the Alcmaeoenids. We know quite a bit about Andocides, not least because a later speech of his on the matter remains on record.[31]

This speech is significant because it is highly probable that the enemies of Alcibiades leaned on Andocides and persuaded him to add an appendix to his confession – namely that at various occasions before the launching of the expedition, Alcibiades and his friends had performed a drunken parody of the rites of the sacred Elusian Mysteries. Exactly what these rites were is, well, a mystery. Some believe that at the rites the goddess Persephone (or a woman personifying the same) returned from her seasonal stay in the underworld to be reunited with her mother Demeter, the corn goddess, and fertility returned to the earth. No one who had been to the Mysteries could confirm or deny this, because the law demanded the death penalty for anyone who revealed what they had seen. Given that this was so, if a convincing case could be made that Alcibiades had profaned the Mysteries with a drunken parody, then he was doomed.

Obviously, Alcibiades had not been alone in his parody, but the accusers cut down the number of those who might perish as collateral damage by putting at the party those already accused of defacing herms and those who had fled the city while the witch-hunt was getting underway. Archaeological evidence confirming this has been found in the form of inscriptions detailing the accused and the confiscation of their property.[32]

Who did and said what and to whom is described in some detail by Andocides in his speech. This detail was necessary as he was attempting by some impressive verbal gymnastics to show that he knew who had defaced the herms and he knew of the parody of the Mysteries, but was still personally completely innocent of any wrongdoing.

Alcibiades' enemies put about a further rumour. The mysterious movements of the Spartans and the arming of the Thebans had only led to nothing because the vigilant citizens of Athens had already seized those aristocratic collaborators of Alcibiades who were to have staged an aristocratic coup in his absence. Had these men not been arrested or driven into exile they would have betrayed the city to its enemies in exchange for being put into power, much in the same way as Alcibiades was doing at that very moment to the oligarchs in Catana.

Public opinion hardened against the city's former golden boy and even his remaining supporters were forced to admit that there was certainly enough *prima facie* testimony against him for Alcibiades to be ordered to return to Athens and face his accusers.

So it was that the *Salamina* came to be in the harbour of Catana with passage for one booked for immediate return to the Piraeus with all due dispatch. Alcibiades boarded ship with a few chosen companions, and in this ignominious fashion the man who had been the driving force behind the Athenian expedition and who had guided events up to this point left Sicily, never to return.

Chapter 5

The Gloves Come Off

We're all in this together. I have more confidence in this army going into battle without a long speech of encouragement that I'd have in a weak army that had just been given a good speech.

> Nicias to the troops immediately before the
> battle of the Olympieum (Thuc. 6.68)

With Alcibiades gone, his diplomatic approach went as well. Lamachus had his own means of persuasion, and with the Lamachus method ships and hoplites spoke louder than words. The expedition had come to Sicily ostensibly to help the Egestans against the Selinans. Very well. Let that be the first order of business. Although both Lamachus and Nicias agreed that Egesta should get the thirty talents of military support the city had paid for, they were sufficiently divided about how to go about this that they split the expedition into two, with each general commanding one half. This done, both halves proceeded towards Egesta as separate commands.

Thus to the bemusement of the Syracusans, the fleet threatening them sailed off westward along the north coast of Sicily and did not return until the end of summer. This left the people of the city free to complete their preparations for an Athenian attack at their leisure, although some returned to the belief that it was all a waste of time. The Syracusans' brief attack of panic had been again replaced with complacency, now somewhat tinged with contempt. They felt it was clear that, despite the rantings of Hermocrates, all Athens and the grand expedition intended to achieve was a propaganda show and a limited military action in support of Egesta on the other side of Sicily.

In fact Nicias had gone west with the intention not just of making war on Selinus, but also of screwing out of Egesta every drachma that the city could afford in payment for that service. To concentrate minds on the Egestan city council, Nicias arrived with half the Athenian fleet and the implicit threat that non-payment would result in Egesta rather than Selinus being attacked. The Egestans paid up.

While Nicias was shaking down Egesta for its promised contribution, Lamachus demonstrated the willingness of the Athenians to keep their side of the bargain. He led a competent attack on Hyccara, a small city allied to Selinus. Once the Athenians had stormed the strong point they loaded the inhabitants of the city on to the fleet and shipped them back to Catana. There the conquered men, women and children were sold as slaves. In this way the expedition raised 150 talents, which meant that, combined with cash contributions from friendly Italian cities, Nicias could report that Athens had made a healthy operating profit of some 400 talents over the early months.[33]

Having given up the hoplite berths in the fleet for their newly enslaved prisoners, the generals took the army back to Catana overland. This route gave the Athenians the chance to impress and negotiate with the Sicels of the interior. The support of these people was seen as increasingly important, as it was evident that the Athenians would find few friends among the Sicilian Greeks. As further proof of this, the only city along the Athenians' route to Egesta was Himera, and the Himerans adamantly refused to have anything to do with the Athenians.

As might be expected of a people who had a large army passing through their midst, the Sicels were inclined to be diplomatic. They did not refuse to countenance the Athenian suggestion that they raise an army to begin ridding themselves of the Greek colonies on their shores, but they did not immediately begin raising that army either.

It was evident that a further Athenian demonstration of force was required to inspire potential allies and deter potential enemies. The generals picked the small town of Hybala in the south-eastern interior as their next victim. Presumably, the town was chosen because of its location halfway between Syracuse and Camerina. A successful action would worry the Syracusans, as the Athenians were operating close to their city, and for the same reason overawe the Camerinans whom the Athenians still hoped to win over. It would also demonstrate to the Sicels that the Athenians could operate away from the coast. We are told that only half the forces of the expedition were involved, and can guess that this half was commanded by Lamachus. In any case, the attack failed, leaving Camerinans, Syracusans and Sicels even less impressed with the Athenians than they had been before.

By now the news was also getting about that the Athenians had mislaid Alcibiades. In theory their scapegrace general was not under arrest, but merely requested home to discuss the charges laid against him. By force of personality, Alcibiades impressed on captain and crew of the *Salamina* that he was a passenger who had boarded the ship voluntarily, and they had no right to treat him as a prisoner. Therefore when the *Salamina* docked at the Italian town of Thurii on its homeward journey Alcibiades insisted, as would any aristocrat on a similar voyage, on leaving the ship to pay his respects to the local noblemen.

Throughout Greece in this period the idea of *xenia*, or guest-friendship, was an essential part of international relations. Every Greek city had noblemen with ties of friendship to other cities, and this nobleman was expected to entertain aristocratic guests from those cities when they came calling. For an Athenian of the stature of Alcibiades not to pay his respects to the aristocrats of Thurii while he was in the area would be an insult only explicable if Alcibiades were a prisoner, which he was not.

After all, Alcibiades had also left the ship when it called at Messene, and had obediently returned afterwards. Later it turned out that Alcibiades had been plotting in Messene, and his allies were on the point of turning the city over to the Athenians. Now the vindictive Alcibiades used his final visit to meet with the pro-Syracusan party in Messene. He informed them of the conspiracy and turned over enough information to make sure that the plot came to nothing.

The crew of the *Salamina* was unaware that Alcibiades had already turned traitor in Messene and so let him and his retinue off the ship at Thurii to do their diplomatic duty. Alcibiades did not return, and though the crew of the *Salamina* turned the city upside down looking for him, they eventually had to sail leaving him behind. When one of Alcibiades' new hosts asked him, 'So, you can't trust even your own country?' Alcibiades remarked ruefully that: 'I wouldn't even trust my own mother not to cast her vote for my death.'

Quite possibly that is exactly what Alcibiades' mother did. Certainly after hearing that he had gone missing the Athenians promptly sentenced Alcibiades to death *in absentia*. When he heard the news, the condemned man is reported to have growled, 'Well then. I'll have to show them that I'm alive.'[34]

Prelude to battle
The Athenian failure either to hold on to Alcibiades or to take Hybala persuaded the Syracusans that the vaunted enemy expedition was in fact a paper tiger. Pressure grew on the city's generals for Syracuse to take the initiative and kick the Athenians out of Sicily altogether. Syracuse, like Athens, was a democracy (incidentally giving the lie to the modern myth that democracies do not make war on each other) and consequently popular pressure would translate into action, however unwise the Syracusan leaders thought that action might be.

It was not that the Syracusans were inexperienced at war – military training and actual combat were regular events in the life of any able-bodied Greek male. However, those actions that the Syracusans had fought recently were small-scale stuff, such as the takeover of little Leontini. This hardly qualified the Syracusan phalanx to take on the battle-hardened and very experienced Athenians, and the commanders on both sides knew it.

But the Syracusan voters wanted a battle, and they would have it, so the generals on both sides planned accordingly. Because the Athenians had failed to bring over the Sicels and cities of Sicily to their side, their expedition was almost totally without cavalry. This was a major problem, because if the Athenians wanted to pick a good battlefield, they would have to march to it. On the march, the hoplites would undoubtedly be harassed by Syracusan light troops. There was no chance of throwing these light troops back with Athenian skirmishers, because the Syracusans had cavalry, and cavalry sufficient to make mincemeat of any Athenian light troops who strayed too far from the protective hedge of the phalanx's spears. This had already been made clear by light troops who had landed in Syracusan farmland to do a day's forage and pillaging. The Syracusan cavalry had caught them at it and handled them roughly – a minor victory that had again boosted Syracusan confidence.

Nor could the Athenians take ship to somewhere suitable near Syracuse and disembark to fight there. The triremes would be spotted while still well off shore, and the landing would undoubtedly be disputed. A difficult battle would result before even a beach-head could be established, leaving the Athenians in poor shape for the major battle to follow. So it seemed as though the Athenians would have to wait for the Syracusans to come to them and fight their battle at a time and a place of the enemy's choosing.

The Athenians had resigned themselves to this fact, a pro-Syracusan defector from Catana informed the Syracusan council. The army of the expedition was currently quartered in Catana and, presumably to prevent the issues that occur naturally when soldiers, wine and swords are together within a strange city, the Athenian hoplites slept well away from where their weapons were stored. Were the Syracusans to arrive unexpectedly at dawn, a fifth column within the city would ensure that the gates were open. Saboteurs were already in place, ready to have the Athenian ships torched at the same time. In the chaos the Syracusans could fall on the confused and disorganized Athenians and end the crisis at a blow.

That this plan of action was adopted so enthusiastically by the Syracusan generals reflects a naivety long lost by those who had to fight the wily

Athenians on a more regular basis. Had (for example) a more cynical Spartan general been on hand, he would have pointed out that sitting back and waiting on events was not the Athenian way. The 'pro-Syracusan defector' might be all the more convincing because he was describing pretty much what the Syracusan generals would have done in Nicias's position, but the Athenians tended to be proactive in military affairs, and simply did not surrender the initiative so tamely.

The Syracusan journey up the learning curve of warfare against Athens began when the first units of cavalry arrived at Catana just before daybreak. Contrary to expectations, they found the city gates firmly barred against them and the walls defended from attack. As the cavalry returned to inform the main army that their surprise attack wasn't, the horsemen made a yet more disconcerting discovery. The Athenian fleet had also been up before dawn. Now, silhouetted against the sunrise, were ships packed with hoplites heading south, certain to reach Syracuse before the home army could execute a smart about-face and head back to their city at full speed.

Fortunately for the city, Syracuse had too many other enemies to leave the walls totally undefended even when they assumed their principal foe was snugly abed in Catana. The scratch garrison manning the city's defences might not be able to hold out long, but they could certainly resist for the few hours it took for their army to hurry back home. The Athenians knew this, and while it would have been pleasant to find the city wide open, realistic expectations were limited to their original intention – to fight a battle near Syracuse on ground of their own choosing, without the hoplites from the fleet having to make an opposed landing.

The chosen battleground was at the Olympieum, an area outside the Syracusan city walls near the south shore of the Great Harbour. The Great Harbour was a roughly kidney-shaped bay about a mile and a half long and a mile across at the widest. Only the north-east side of this bay abutted the walls of the city, these walls being the fortified 'island' and causeway of Ortygia where the Syracusans had first settled. The rest of the city stretched northward along the gentle slopes of a hill in an area called Achradina, while the uninhabited western shores of the Great Harbour were occupied by a marsh formed where the river Anapus flowed into the sea. (It was this marsh – *siraco* – which is believed to have given the city of Syracuse its name.) The main feature of the Olympieum was the great temple of Olympian Zeus, a temple loaded with consecrated offerings of gold and silver. Nicias was a pious man and had no designs on this treasure, but the Syracusans could not be certain of this, and would be all the more eager to give battle to stop the

Athenians taking the bullion from the temple into protective custody. (The remains of the temple of the Olympieum are known in modern Syracuse as Le Colonne – columns amid a modern urban backdrop.)

The Athenians began by landing south of the marsh and then made their way north on the higher ground behind it. They stopped on the slopes overlooking the Anapus river and took the time to demolish the bridge on the Syracuse–Gela road, which went over that river. The entire area was closed in by marsh, houses and woodland. The only point where cavalry could make themselves useful was in a small area on the Athenian army's seaward flank, so, since the Syracusans were only expected home in the late afternoon, the Athenians spent a leisurely day fortifying this sole vulnerable point.

Nicias was in charge, which explained why the Athenians were leaving nothing to chance. Lamachus might have simply noted that man-for-man the Athenians were better soldiers than the Syracusans, and therefore fought his battle on more-or-less even terms. Nicias, being Nicias, wanted to shorten his odds. Therefore he had arranged it so that the Syracusans would arrive home late having set out well before dawn. They had marched about halfway to Catana. Then they had turned around and marched – somewhat faster – all the way back. Many Athenian hoplites had walked less than half a mile all day and were rested and fresh. Nevertheless, Nicias wanted the Syracusans to have to ford the river Anapus and then charge uphill against his army, which was properly formed in an area where the Syracusans could get no advantage from their cavalry. Soldiers might have loved Lamachus for his derring-do, but they appreciated the care Nicias took with their lives.

The Battle of the Olympieum[35]

The Syracusan cavalry were first at the scene. They reconnoitred the carefully prepared battleground and reported back to the main army, which arrived as dusk was falling. The Syracusan generals were no fools. They knew that the Athenians were rested and their own men were tired. They also knew that with their army now between the Athenians and Syracuse, the city was in no danger. There was only one reason to risk a battle, and that was because the morale of the army might suffer if the generals were seen to hold back.

A hoplite battle was very much between consenting parties. Siege warfare in the fifth century was a relatively primitive affair and it was difficult even to take a well-situated camp by storm. The usual way of getting an armed force out of a defensive position was to block access to food and water until the enemy had no choice but to come out and fight. So if there was to be a battle that evening it would be because generals on the Athenian and Syracusan side both wanted one.

So the Syracusans offered battle, but on their own terms. They advanced towards the Athenian army but did not close with it. Presumably the intention was to tempt the Athenians off the higher ground and over the river so that the battle would be fought on more even terms. If the Athenians did this, then the enthusiasm of the Syracusan soldiers might counter their weariness from their long march that day. If Nicias refused to give up his advantageous position (and this was a pretty good bet), then the Syracusans could retire for the night knowing that it was the Athenians who had declined battle, and therefore morale in their army would remain high. Sure enough, Nicias declined the offer to come out and fight, so the Syracusan army pulled back and both sides prepared for battle on the morrow.

This battle was significant as it was to be the first full trial of strength between the armies. No really decisive outcome was likely. If defeated the Syracusans could fall back on their city and the Athenians on their fleet, so each side could escape relatively unscathed. However, the victor would demonstrate to the cities of Sicily which side was the better in the open field, and therefore which would make the better ally. It might have occurred to those neutrals in Sicily that they were like ewes in a field watching the Syracusan ram butting heads with the Athenian for the right to their favours.

Nicias knew this was the reason for the battle, and as the armies drew up the next day he warned his soldiers: 'There is no friendly territory here in Sicily unless we fight and win it over … we are fighting for a country that is not ours, and if we lose there will be no safe place to hide.' Having given his men dire warnings about the perils of defeat, Nicias then pointed out the obvious – there was no reason to expect anything but victory. The Athenians and their allies were picked men with hard-won battle experience. The Syracusans were basically enthusiastic beginners.

The core of the expeditionary force was the 1,500 veteran Athenian hoplites Nicias put at the centre of the battle line. The volunteers from Argos who had accompanied Alcibiades were put on the right wing, together with a motley mix of other freebooters (many from Mantinea) and mercenaries. The rest of the Athenian battle line was made up of levies from subject cities of the Athenian empire. It was probably for the latter's benefit that Nicias had stressed the perils of defeat. The levies had no reason to fight hard for an Athenian victory, but defeat would leave them no less exposed to Syracusan vengeance than the Athenians.

Once assembled, the battle line filled all the space available between hills and marsh, which was exactly as Nicias wanted it, since he had no desire to see enemy cavalry on his flanks when he had none of his own with which to counter. In fact, after deploying his men in ranks eight deep, Nicias had half his army left over. This he deployed in a hollow square about his supplies and non-combatants, both as a strategic reserve and as a guard should part of his line buckle and the Syracusan cavalry break through the gap.

Veteran general and veteran soldiers organized themselves with minimal fuss and immediately advanced on the Syracusan camp. This caused consternation on the Syracusan side, as the Sicilians were accustomed to a more protracted lead-in to their battles. In fact, some Syracusan hoplites who had taken the opportunity to pop into the city for a quick breakfast had to come racing back, grab their weapons and rush straight into their battle line. This line consequently formed up as a single, slightly disorganized, phalanx of 5,000-6,000 men, sixteen ranks deep, with the cavalry milling about behind that.

The weather was oppressive, with heavy grey clouds overhead. The clash of the skirmishers on both sides was punctuated by occasional flashes of lightning and grumbling thunder as archers, slingers and stone-throwers advanced and retreated between the facing lines of armoured men, slipping behind their sheltering shields when the enemy pressed hard and rushing out when they faltered. Meanwhile priests and soothsayers on both sides examined the omens and determined whether the gods willed a battle that day. That the signs were favourable was announced by the unmusical but definitely warlike blare of the *salpinx*, a bronze trumpet that had much in common with the modern vuvuzela. This was the signal for the two armies to advance towards each other.

It was traditional for a Greek army advancing into battle to sing the paean, a hymn to the gods whom some participants could expect to meet personally before the day was out. 'The Greeks sing the stately paean ... because they go into battle with brave hearts,' explains the poet.[36] When Greek faced Greek, sometimes each side sang a different version of the paean (the Dorian and Ionian versions were somewhat different) or attempted to drown the other out, but there would have been occasions when the two sides sang the same song together even as their armoured ranks crashed into mortal combat.

The nature of that combat is the topic of a heated debate among military historians. There are basically two schools of thought – the 'scrum' and the 'stab'. Scrummers hold that a hoplite battle was won or lost by those in the rear ranks who literally put their shields to the backs of those on the front line and tried to push them through the ranks of the enemy. Stabbers believe that the two battle lines duelled spear-to-spear until each man had defeated his opposite number. There can be no doubt that shoving played a large part in Greek hoplite warfare. The Greeks even have a word for it – the *othismos*. Sadly, because this was such an integral part of a hoplite battle, none of our sources feel the need to define exactly what it was, just as today no one defines what a 'charge' or an 'encirclement' was.

It is generally agreed by historians that a battle had to be more than a simple shoving match, since any modern rugby modern scrummager will point out that a scrum can be exhausting if sustained for nearly a minute, and some hoplite battles went on for hours. A consensus appears to be forming that a battle might begin with each side having a determined push at the other, and if that failed, settling in to bouts of sparring with spears, interspersed with local pushes if one side or another felt it had the advantage in a particular area. Nevertheless, although for different reasons, both ancient and modern historians agree that battles were highly confused affairs in which no one really knew what was going on or how anyone apart from an immediate opponent was doing (not unlike a modern rugby scrum, in fact). Certainly, the generals had no idea what was happening, for once a general had deployed his troops and given a suitably rousing speech, his job was done. Thereafter he picked up his shield and fought in the ranks like everybody else.

Everyone agrees that the objective of a victorious hoplite army was to break through the battle line of the opposing force. A phalanx with a broken line was as helpless as a turtle upon its back. No longer could the locked shield line protect each warrior, for now peril threatened at the back or the side as well. The only way a man could face that peril was to turn to face it, thus further disrupting the shieldwall and exposing his neighbours to attack from all sides. An army with a broken battle line was a defeated army and everyone knew it, so once a battle line was broken it was every hoplite for himself.

There was a further twist to a battle that made phalanx warfare an even more nerve-wracking affair than it would already be. Those who were first to abandon a lost cause had the best chance of making it off the battlefield alive. Those who stood their ground were doomed to near-certain death or enslavement. So when an enemy shove forced the line back a pace or two, the question that went through every hoplite's mind was whether this was the moment when the line broke. Now, should he try to stand his ground and become a dead hero, or flee and precipitate a rout from which he would at least emerge alive? Just to add to the confusion, our hoplite had no idea whether he and his friends were the only part of the line that was buckling or the last remnants of the army still on the field.

Of course, if everyone stood their ground, the army was safe. At least ninety percent of the casualties in a hoplite action came when one side was running away. However, if anyone was going to run away, the choice for the rest was between an early departure and an early grave.

The only soldiers who did not face this dilemma were the Spartans. A Spartan who fled the battlefield was so disgraced that he might as well commit suicide anyway, so his only choices were between an honourable death in battle or a disgraceful death afterwards. And since a Spartan's fellow hoplites had the same choices, they could be trusted to remain in the battle line with him. Spartan battle lines did not break, which is why the Spartans almost always won.[37]

In the current battle outside Syracuse, the Athenians were confident of victory. Since no one runs away from a winning battle, this made victory all the more certain as local setbacks were ignored. The Syracusans had no such faith in their fellow hoplites, and though their morale was high, it was also fragile. Thucydides now takes up the tale.

> Once the armies had come to grips with each other, for some time neither would give ground. The thunderclaps and lighting flashes were now accompanied by heavy rain. All this unsettled the Syracusans who were fighting their first [major] battle and had generally little experience of warfare. The hoplites on the other side were hardened warriors, and the storm that disturbed their opponents was simply regarded something to be expected at this time of the year. What was causing the Athenian side some apprehension was that the Syracusan line was taking so long to buckle.
>
> It was the Argives on the left who first managed to push the Syracusans back, and then the Athenians broke through the enemy ranks in the centre. Once their line had been cut in two the Syracusans were routed.
>
> Thuc. 6.70

In any ancient battle, this was the moment to unleash the cavalry. The horsemen would thunder down on the fleeing enemy, adding to their panic and cutting them down from behind. Any who turned to organize a defence would instead be cut down by the victorious advancing hoplites. Who survived and who perished or was captured was a matter of chance and of whether any of the advancing army fancied the hoplite *panoply* worn by a fleeing foe. Shields were to be had in abundance, for the heavy *aspis* was the first thing that a warrior abandoned when he took to flight. This was convenient, because after a battle shields doubled as stretchers for bearing away the wounded and dead. (Hence the famous advice of a Spartan mother to her son: 'Come back with your shield, or on it.')

If Nicias now let loose his cavalry, there was a chance that Athenian and Syracusan hoplites would become part of a disorganized mob roiling towards the city gates, leaving those guarding the gate the devil's alternative of either shutting the gates and having their beaten army cut to pieces before the walls, or leaving the gates open for the Athenians to enter the city with the rest of the crowd. But Nicias had no cavalry. Instead the Athenian general watched as some 1,200 Syracusan-horses wheeled into position to cover the Syracusan defeat. If the pursuing Athenians became too disorganized in their headlong rush to catch and kill the broken infantry, the Syracusan cavalry threatened a charge. This forced the Athenians to halt and dress their line while the Syracusan foot continued to retreat pell-mell. The experienced Athenians promptly formed compact blocks, which were invulnerable to any horsemen suicidal enough to attack them, but such blocks could not move as fast as the uninhibited freestyle of the Syracusan infantry retreat. In the end the Athenians gave up the pursuit, fell back and erected a trophy to their victory.

A trophy was important. One made a trophy by stripping the best *panoply* available from its deceased owner and chopping down a tree at just below shoulder height. Then the panoply was mounted on the tree with a spear as the cross bar and the helmet set atop. The trophy (from whence comes the modern word) said: 'The side whose owner once had this *panoply* was clearly and unequivocally defeated.'

In this case the trophy was a message not just for the Syracusans but for all Sicily. All that remained was for the Syracusans now to formally acknowledge their defeat by sending heralds to ask for permission to gather their dead. There were, it turned out, about 260 of these, compared to some fifty dead Athenians and their allies. Such low casualty figures meant that the Athenian victory was purely symbolic. In military terms it affected nothing but the respective morale of the two sides. But as has been seen, in hoplite warfare morale was hugely significant. The Syracusans had been defeated in a fair fight, and therefore could expect to be beaten again, not least because so many more of their warriors were now prepared to flee at the first apparent setback.

Taking stock

Nicias had achieved his objective. He had cowed the enemy, sent a message to the rest of Sicily and had a victory report to send home. Now that the expedition had achieved an impressively solid success, Nicias once again argued passionately that he and the army should be allowed to go home while the going was good.

Certainly there was no question of the Athenians remaining camped where they were outside Syracuse. The Syracusan army had used the protection of their cavalry to good effect and had not even retreated as far as the city walls. They had rallied near the temple of the Olympieum, and now occupied it in case Nicias changed his mind about taking charge of the treasure within. The Athenians would have to fight again if they wanted to pen the Syracusans back within their city walls, and, having made his point, Nicias was not keen on this idea.

Winter if not actually arrived was well on the way, and the Athenians were not yet set up for a drawn-out siege. Whatever happened, the expedition was in Sicily for the next few months, simply because the seas were now too rough for a fleet to attempt a crossing to Greece. Corn needed to be procured, both from allied cities for the winter and probably later from Athens if it was decided that the expedition should keep going through the following summer.

Therefore the hoplites of the expedition re-embarked and sailed back up the coast to Catana. Alcibiades would be badly missed over the coming winter, which may have been a period of military inactivity, but would certainly feature some furious diplomatic activity.

In Syracuse, the citizens had no choice to act as though the Athenians would be back. As the man who had correctly called the course of events to date, Hermocrates had far and away the most credibility of any Syracusan politician. Now, as his enemies had long predicted, Hermocrates used the Athenian threat to make a bid for power.

An assembly of the people was convened. In this Hermocrates pointed out that the Syracusan army had in fact not done too badly considering that they had been a bunch of high-spirited amateurs taking on the second-most-practised army in Greece. Two things had led to defeat – lack of proper training and leadership by committee. The winter gave the Syracusans breathing space for practising drill and weapons training. The state should supply arms to any able-bodied men who lacked them and spend the winter months making these men both disciplined and proficient in warfare.

Secondly, the number of Syracusan commanders should be drastically reduced to three, and this triumvirate should be given a great deal more power than the generals currently exercised. This would allow the city to react promptly to emergencies and also for the generals to keep their plans secret from the enemy. Obviously, the three should be men able to work well together, and their leading light should be a man who had shown early that he appreciated the threat posed by the Athenians and long urged action to counter it. Such a man as himself, for example. The Syracusans took the hint and overwhelmingly voted Hermocrates and his friends near-dictatorial powers.

Two of the last triremes of the sailing season were sent on the pre-winter crossing to Greece. Both asked for help from the mainland. The Athenian trireme bore news of the victory outside the walls of Syracuse, and Nicias's recommendation that the expedition had achieved the best result it could get and that it should now be recalled. The Syracusan trireme was bound for Sparta, where ambassadors would urge their fellow Dorians to take the war to Athens on the Greek mainland. Then the Syracusan delegation would travel on to Corinth to urge that city to come to the aid of its colony and recall the numerous grudges the Corinthians had against the Athenian state and people.

Then, with the triremes dispatched, both sides turned their attention to wooing the peoples and cities of Sicily. First stop for the Athenians was Messene. The Athenians had been in constant communication with the democratic element in the city, and were confident that their victory outside Syracuse would provide the final stimulus for a democratic revolution. The expedition commanders were until then unaware that the final act of Alcibiades on the island had been to carefully unravel the plot by giving the oligarchic rulers of Messene chapter and verse of by whom, where and when the uprising was planned.

As soon as they heard that the Athenians were on the way, the oligarchic faction arrested and executed the democratic ringleaders, and used the turmoil that this provoked to bring the city under martial law. Thus the Athenian fleet arrived to find Messene under military occupation and the gates barred against them. For almost two weeks the fleet hung hopefully around the harbour of Messene in the hope that their presence might yet be the catalyst for revolution. But the betrayal by Alcibiades had been too comprehensive for any survivor to raise the banner of rebellion. It eventually dawned on the disillusioned Athenians that they were wasting their time. The expedition moved on to Naxos with the intention of wintering there, in one of only two cities that had come over to their cause.

As soon as he heard that the Athenians were at Naxos, Hermocrates pulled a scratch force together and attacked the Athenian encampment at Catana.

The encampment was empty, but the Syracusans gained a certain satisfaction from burning the Athenian tents and capturing whatever supplies they could find or loot from the surrounding countryside.

This minor military action was the last of the year. Though it amounted to a pinprick in military terms, it reminded the rest of Sicily that Syracuse was still active and aggressive. This was to be of considerable value in the winter diplomacy to come.

Chapter Six

The Siege of Syracuse

The defenders of the city, scared as fawns, wiped away the sweat from their bodies as they leaned against their trusty battlements, while below the Greeks put their shields to their shoulders and closed up on the walls.

Homer, *Iliad* 22.1

The power of persuasion

Thucydides summarizes the winter of diplomacy in Sicily with a case study of a debate between Syracusans and Athenian ambassadors at Camerina. This small south-eastern city was both pro-Athenian and an ally of Syracuse, and both sides were determined to pull Camerina off the fence and make it declare for one side or the other. The arguments used in this debate were probably used in the other cities of Sicily, albeit with regional variations. Therefore these are worth describing here.

The Syracusans were represented by Hermocrates himself. The Syracusan leader poured scorn on the idea that the Athenians had come to Sicily to defend the independence of cities such as Leontini and Egesta: 'As if the Athenians cared so much about the freedom of the people of Leontini, who are colonists from Chalcis … when the Athenians have actually subjugated Chalcis itself.' Hermocrates claimed – with considerable justification – that the Athenians had come not to restore the people of Leontini to their own, but to take for themselves what was not theirs. 'Just as they won an empire over in Hellas, they are trying to win another one here, and in exactly the same way.' Those who joined with Athens against Persia had not ended up with the freedom they were fighting for. Instead they had exchanged the tolerant and easygoing Persian rule for 'smarter and more evil' masters.

Were the people of Sicily so unintelligent, wondered Hermocrates aloud, that even with the past record of Athenian misdeeds plainly before them, they would fall for the same tricks that had worked for the Athenians in the past? Would they not see that the Athenians intended to take over Sicily city-by-city, allying with one here, conquering another here, installing a pro-Athenian government there, until the whole island was in their power? In short, was anyone so foolish as to imagine that this was a fight between Athens and Syracuse alone?

This was particularly the case for Camerina, since this small city was on the borders of Syracuse. The Athenians might claim to be best friends with Camerina now, but if they defeated Syracuse they would find Camerina's earlier neutrality a cause for war in the future. Hermocrates did not remind the Camerinans that neutrality had not helped Melos, possibly because the event was notorious enough not to need further mention. Indeed, Hermocrates next went on to say there was no point in explaining to the people of Camerina 'things that you already know just as well as we do'. He wrapped up his speech with a final sting.

> If you betray us, and the Athenians overcome us, they will owe their conquest to your decision. However, make no mistake, they will take all the credit for the victory. And as a prize they will reward themselves with mastery over you, the very people who helped them win. On the other hand if the victory goes to us, you are hardly going to escape the consequences for putting us in danger. So think carefully and choose – instant slavery without risk, or a chance to save yourselves by fighting with us.

Since the Syracusan case basically explained the strategy of Alcibiades in careful detail, the Athenians required a good speaker for their rebuttal. And that's exactly what Euphemus, the name of the Athenian representative, means: 'Eu', good; 'phanai', speak.

Euphemus made no attempt to disguise the fact that Athens had won itself an empire and no effort to disguise how this had been done. But the Athenian motive was not imperialism for its own sake, as Hermocrates had implied – it was self-defence. On the one side the Ionians faced the expansionist Persian Empire and on the other the warlike Dorian peoples of the Peloponnese. All that the Athenians could do was to unite the Ionians under their leadership and so keep their city free. Yes, they had to subjugate some Ionians to do this, but these were Ionians already subjugated by Persia: 'The fact is that these kinsmen of ours joined the Persians in attacking their mother city.'

The Athenians had built their island empire out of fear of more powerful foes, Euphemus claimed. Now that same fear had brought them to Sicily. He admitted that the Athenians were expert in cajoling and coercing cities into an alliance with them. Consequently, when someone else was playing the same game, no one could see it better than the Athenians. What Hermocrates was doing was casting the Athenians in the role of Persia, so that Syracuse could play the Athenian game and unite the cities of Sicily under Syracusan leadership. It would be easy to become allies of Syracuse, Euphemus admitted. But would it be anywhere near as easy to leave that alliance?

What had brought Athens to Sicily was Syracusan expansionism. The conquest of little Leontini was the first step in uniting Sicily under Syracusan rule, and this frankly scared the Athenians. Athens had its hands full coping with a hostile Asia Minor ruled by the Persians and a hostile Peloponnese ruled by the Spartans. A hostile Sicily ruled by Syracuse was one threat too many. The Athenians had come to divide, not to conquer.

> We are guided by our own best interests here. The Syracusans intend to rule over you. The plan is to make you so suspicious of us that they can create a Sicilian empire … We originally came here because we were asked by cities afraid of falling under the power of Syracuse, and they said that if we allowed Syracuse to take control [of the island], we would be in danger. So it is hardly fair to condemn us now for the very reasons that you wanted us over here in the first place.

If Hermocrates had neatly summarized the arguments of Alcibiades and his supporters, Euphemus could respond with the Nicias viewpoint.

> Even if we were evil enough to try to enslave you, we couldn't. We have enormously long lines of communication, and we would have to use these to garrison cities as powerful as any in mainland Greece.

Now Syracuse, on the other hand (Euphemus continued), was perfectly situated to build a Sicilian empire. Their city was right there, and their army was larger. They had a proven record of meddling in other Sicilian cities' affairs and picking off weaker neighbours when they could. Yet those same Syracusans were now asking Camerina to fight alongside them against the very people who had come to prevent them from being victims of Syracuse's plans for a Sicilian empire.

Euphemus summarized thus. In Greece, Athens had built an empire by coercion and diplomatic manoeuvre. This was necessary to preserve the freedom of the city. In Sicily, Syracuse was trying to build an empire by coercion and diplomatic manoeuvre. This empire would be used by pro-Spartan Syracuse against Athens. Therefore, to preserve the freedom of Athens, it was necessary to stop Syracuse. There was no inconsistency in subjugating cities close to Athens while fighting for the independence of other cities more distant. In each case the objective was the same – the freedom of Athens.

The Camerinans should choose their side without reference to rhetoric or emotional appeals. Athens and Syracuse were both acting out of self-interest, and Camerina should do the same. Both Athens and Syracuse accused each other of empire-building. Now seriously, which city was the more immediate danger?

The people of Camerina were torn. Syracuse was their neighbour, and, unlike the Athenians, there was no chance of the Syracusans ever going away. On the other hand, the Camerinans rather liked the Athenians, and the Athenians had just handily trounced the Syracusans in battle. In the end, the city announced to both sides that they were currently allies of each, and would like to remain that way. If either Athens or Syracuse withdrew from their alliance with Camerina, by default Camerina would be on the other side. Until then, Camerina was not going to get involved.[38]

As diplomats from both sides toured the island through the winter trying to recruit other cities into their war they repeatedly encountered variations on the Camerinan response. Neither Athens nor Syracuse was considered an ally trustworthy enough to be worth fighting for.

If the cites of Sicily were not budging from the fence, other ambassadors had more luck. Both sides worked hard for the hearts and minds of the Sicels. The Athenians seem to have used the tried-and-trusted maxim that 'the enemy of my enemy is my friend'. Now that the Syracusans had been beaten in battle, the Sicels of the interior responded enthusiastically. Syracuse was a clear and present danger to their independence, and even if Athens did gain control of Sicily and become an enemy, an enemy based hundreds of miles away was better than one right beside them.

Therefore the Athenians obtained volunteers, corn and money from friendly Sicel tribes and help in coercing those tribes who were not friendly. They had less success with Sicels nearer the coast, as the Syracusans posted garrisons in these tribal areas. The garrisons served both as a disincentive to Sicels planning to rise against Syracuse and to prevent the Athenians from forcing the Sicels to do so.

Diplomats abroad

Other ambassadors went even further afield. The Athenians made goodwill visits to Carthage and Etruria to see how much anti-Syracusan feeling they

View of Athenian tombs near the Keremaikos. Here Greeks who fell in battle were buried in an annual ceremony. Every effort was made to retrieve corpses from a battlefield and bring them home to Athens. (Photograph courtesy of Jeremy Day)

Temple at Egesta on Sicily. This construction is contemporary with the Athenian expedition, and indeed it may be that the elements of the temple which are incomplete are so because building work was overtaken by the events described in this book. (Photograph courtesy of Jeremy Day)

Modern view of the Syracuse harbour from Epipolae via the Euryalus Pass, with Plemmyrium at the top right of the picture. (Photograph courtesy of Dr Nigel Pollard)

The remains of the Temple of Apollo in Syracuse. Enough of the building has survived to show the early Doric design, with possible Ionic influences. (Photograph courtesy of Dr Nigel Pollard)

Part of the peripteros of the temple of Athena on Ortygia in Syracuse, now incorporated into the body of the Duomo (cathedral). (Photograph courtesy of Dr Nigel Pollard)

The quarries at Syracuse where the Athenian prisoners ended their days. (Photograph courtesy of Jeff Champion)

A fragment of stone relief from the Parthenon, the best contemporary evidence of how rowers sat in a trireme. (Photograph Philip Matyszak)

The *Olympias* under way – this is very probably how triremes looked while making long ocean crossings. The mixture of people sitting and standing on the upper decks had to be carefully arranged to keep the ship stable. (Photograph courtesy of The Trireme Trust)

The head-on ram shows the area of the bows where the Syracusans reinforced the cat's heads (top either side of ram) to make their ships less seaworthy but better than the Athenians in a close-quarter head-to-head. Note that usually a ship rigged for action had the sail removed. (Photograph courtesy of The Trireme Trust)

Close up of a trireme's ram cutting through the water. This view is the last thing a rower on the lower deck of an opposing trireme would have seen before all hell broke loose. (Photograph courtesy of The Trireme Trust)

Corinthian-style hoplite helmet. Though many late-fifth-century Greeks preferred the more open style Thracian helmet, this remained a popular form of head protection – and is the type with which Pericles preferred to be depicted. (Photography by Philip Matyszak)

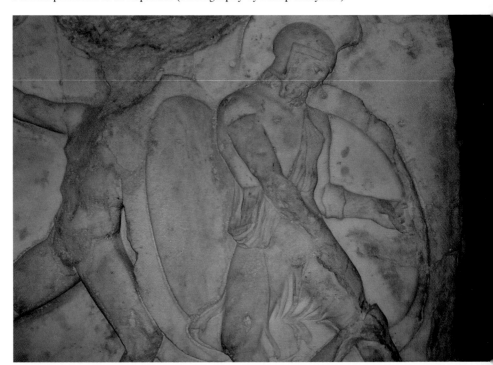

Hoplite in action. This Parthenon bas-relief clearly shows both the interior and the arm-grip of the interior of the hoplite's shield. (Photography by Philip Matyszak)

Hoplite demonstrating overrarm thrust (Photograph courtesy of Mark Harch of the Roman Military Research Society)

Frontal view of hoplite employing overrarm spear thrust. This clearly illustrates the excellent protection offered by the large shield. (Photograph courtesy of Mark Hatch RMRS)

Hoplite re-enactor demonstrating how the sauroter, the spike on the butt end of the spear shaft, can be used to strike down at a fallen opponent. (Photograph courtesy of Mark Hatch RMRS)

Hoplite re-enactor, clearly showing the recurved blade of the *kopis* sword and the grip arrangement of the shield. (Photograph courtesy of Mark Hatch RMRS)

Hoplite re-enactor thrusting over the rim of his shield. (Photograph courtesy of Mark Hatch RMRS)

Hoplite re-enactor at ease, with the Corinthian helmet pushed on to the back of the head for ease of vision and breathing. (Photograph courtesy of Mark Hatch RMRS)

could stir up in each region. In fact both Etruscans and Carthaginians were already keen to see Syracuse crushed, but each had their own ideas of how to go about it. Like the Greeks, the Etruscans lived in city states that frequently warred with one another. Therefore though several spontaneously offered to declare war on Syracuse, fear of their immediate neighbours meant that they could devote few resources to a faraway conflict. In the end only some three or so shiploads of Etruscan warriors turned up later to support the Athenian cause the following spring.

The Carthaginians were politically united, and had a large army that they were ready to use. However, they were playing a different game, and saw little point in helping one lot of Greeks beat up another equally annoying lot of Greeks. Rather, Carthage planned to watch and hoard its resources while Athens and Syracuse fought it out. Once the dust had settled, Carthage intended to execute its own plans for Sicily, especially if the fight had left the winner severely weakened. In short, Carthage intended nothing but harm for Greeks of any persuasion. Consequently, the city encouraged the Athenian ambassadors to continue the fight and to devote all possible resources to it, but they themselves stayed well clear of the war – for now.

If the Athenian ambassadors enjoyed limited success in their excursions abroad, Syracusan ambassadors did a lot better in the Greek homeland itself. One of the first ports of call was Corinth. Corinth had little love for Athens in any case and was determined to give Syracuse all possible support – although as the Spartans had already discovered, 'all possible support' usually stopped short of actually getting involved in bloodshed. And in fact it turned out that the Corinthians intended to support Syracuse's ambassadors by getting behind them in urging Sparta to do the fighting.

The Spartan leaders received the mixed Syracusan–Corinthian delegation without much enthusiasm. The recent clash with Athens had not gone well, and though the current peace more resembled low-tempo warfare, it was better than the full-scale variety. Nevertheless, despite their scepticism, the Spartans listened carefully to an unexpected advocate for the Syracusan cause – Alcibiades of Athens.

Alcibiades had made his way to Sparta. Once there, he deeply impressed the inhabitants by becoming more Spartan than the Spartans. 'He was all for physical exercise, a simple lifestyle and a humourless expression,' remarks Plutarch. 'Seeing him with untrimmed hair in a cold bath, or slurping down black broth [the notoriously ghastly Spartan national dish], or getting familiar with coarse bread, it was hard to imagine that the man once had an in-house chef and personal perfumer.'[1] Alcibiades' passion for all things Spartan included Timaea, wife of the Spartan king Agis. With Agis out of town on state business, Alcibiades filled in for the absent king in the royal bedchamber. There he continued his Spartan studies so enthusiastically that Timaea became pregnant. Later Alcibiades was to claim that his intentions toward Timaea were almost noble, in that he planned not a tawdry affair but to insert a child of his own into the line of the Spartan kings. But for an inconvenient earthquake, he would have succeeded. Just before his departure to foreign parts, Agis had been shaken out of his wife's arms by a mild earthquake. From the moment the earth had moved for him he had – presumably for religious reasons – abstained from sex with his wife. The child was born ten months after this, and the Spartans were quick to do the math.

But for the moment Alcibiades' forthcoming disgrace was no more than an easily hidden bump beneath the queen's robes, and the Spartans were unaware that their Athenian convert was anything less than altruistic. The ex-general laid out the Athenian masterplan for the conquest of Sicily for the edification of the Spartan people, and took care to emphasize that this was but step one in a programme of conquest that would go on to include Carthage, Italy and, ultimately, Sparta. Alcibiades warned that the time to stop the Athenians was before they took Syracuse. True, Syracuse was well armed, prosperous and vigorously defended. But the Syracusans had no idea of what they were up against. The Athenian energy and initiative that had combined with hard-won military experience to trounce the Syracusans on the battlefield would now be applied to the forthcoming siege of the city. Alcibiades confidently expected the Syracusans to be outwitted, outmanoeuvred and outfought. If the city and its people were not helped, an Athenian victory was a matter of time.

Syracuse did not lack resources or enthusiastic defenders. What the city needed was someone to use them to best advantage – someone who knew Athenian strategy and stratagems from years spent on the receiving end of both. In short, Syracuse needed a Spartan general. Alcibiades proposed that Sparta dispatch a trireme with hoplites as rowers, and captained by an experienced commander. Once in Sicily, the hoplites would exchange oars for spears, and the commander would take over the anti-Athenian war effort.

The Spartans listened to this advice and decided it was good. The commander they selected was Gylippus, the son of Cleandridas. Because of a scandal that involved Cleandridas taking bribes from Pericles, Gylippus had spent time in Magna Graecia, where his father had fled to avoid Spartan justice. Since the son was innocent of wrongdoing, he had returned to Sparta, and there received the standard (i.e. abominably harsh) upbringing of a

Spartan child. This upbringing would have been even harder on Gylippus if it is true that he was a *mothax*. *Mothaces* were members of Sparta's semi-slave helot population who were brought up with Spartan children in a family that had adopted them. The father of Gylippus was certainly no helot – until his disgrace he had been an advisor to the king of Sparta. However, the mother may have been, as may have been a grandparent.[39]

Though this would have led to even more intense bullying than normal (in Sparta bullying was seen as another way of building moral fibre in the bullied), being a *mothax* also led to the support and patronage of the Spartan general Lysander, who was himself a *mothax*. Gylippus immediately asked the Corinthians to supply him with two triremes and began making energetic preparations for crossing to Syracuse as soon as winter released its grip on the seaways of the Mediterranean.

Meanwhile, in Sicily both sides had been busy. Nicias had moved the army to Naxos for the winter. There was general criticism of Nicias for allowing the raid of Hermocrates to burn the remnants of the base left behind at Catana. The general theme of the complaints was that Nicias was a highly capable general once he had to fight, but tended to be torpid and uninspired if action was not forced upon him. One of the last ships from Athens before winter had brought twenty-five talents of silver, and the Nicias and Lamachus now put the money to good use in paying for the construction of siege equipment and bribing Sicel leaders. An urgent appeal to Athens had asked for as much cavalry as the city could send, for money to pay the troops already in Sicily and for more to be sent.

The start of the campaigning season in Sicily would see the arrival of several hundred cavalrymen from Athens, including horse archers (presumably Scythian). Another 300 cavalry were expected from Egesta and over a hundred more from Naxos and elsewhere. The Athenians were also sending more ships and 300 talents of silver. The Spartans were sending Gylippus. The balance was hardly equal, but it was the Spartan contribution that would tip the scales tin the end.

Spring 414 BC

Spring in Syracuse brought rain showers and carpets of wild flowers in the fields around the city. The wild flowers were particularly abundant that year. No one was doing much ploughing, for spring also brought the Athenians, and the Athenians brought with them a grim conviction that the time for diplomatic sparring was over. The Athenians intended to get right down to business. They had already started with a cruise down the coast, attacking

Syracusan strong points, burning the winter-wheat crops of unfriendly cities and terrorizing uncooperative Sicel communities. Then the army, including the new cavalry reinforcements from Athens, re-embarked in their ships and set sail for Syracuse.

The Athenian fleet moored at the Thapsus peninsula (see map) in a beautiful little bay which is today a popular bathing spot for Syracusans on weekend breaks. The peninsula was almost uninhabited and seemed a good spot for an Athenian camp. It was some 7 miles north west of Syracuse itself, and was now preferable to the previous landing site near the Olympieum. There, with perfect hindsight, the Syracusans had fortified the area to prevent the Athenians from returning, and while they were at it they had built a stockade most of the way around the Great Harbour.

What happened next perfectly demonstrated the difference between the Syracusan and Athenian armies, and explains why Gylippus made such a difference when he arrived. Most of Syracuse was built on the slope of Achradina, to the north of the Great Harbour. Overlooking Achradina, and now between the Athenian army and the city, were the imposing heights of Epipolae, a steep plateau some 1.8 miles across (*epipolae* means 'plateau'). The more thoughtful type of Syracusan now eyed these heights with the uneasy thought that it would be a very bad thing if the Athenians managed to establish themselves there. Not only would the Athenians actually overlook the city walls, but with Epipolae captured, Athens would be well on the way to cutting Syracuse off from the rest of Sicily. Hermocrates, now in charge of the defence of Syracuse, decided that the passages leading to the heights should not only be garrisoned but garrisoned by a body of some 600 hand-picked men. He duly picked those men and paraded them for review 3 miles to the south of the heights in the meadows alongside the river Anapus.

While this parade was going on, possibly to the accompaniment of stirring speeches stressing the importance of the duty the garrison would be undertaking, the Athenian army marched swiftly out of camp. Proceeding at the double, the Athenian hoplites made straight for the most crucial passage up Epipolae and seized the heights. After a stunned pause and a moment to regroup, the discomfited Syracusan force left the meadows. They marched straight to Epipolae and gamely tried to reclaim the positions where they should have been in the first place. The picked men showed their worth, for almost half the 600 were killed in their furious assault. The Syracusans even threw their vaunted cavalry into the attack, despite the hazard of using horsemen against well-entrenched spearmen, but to no avail. The experienced Athenian hoplites had the better position and had no intention of relinquishing it. The surviving Syracusans had to fall back and eventually acknowledged the loss of the heights by sending a herald to ask for permission to gather their dead.

Even as the Syracusans collected the corpses of their fallen warriors, they could see the Athenians busily constructing fortifications on Epipolae, the better to hold their camp gear and money when they were operating elsewhere. And indeed, as soon as the temporary truce had expired, the Athenians moved again, this time drawing up their army outside the city and inviting the Syracusans to fight a decisive battle. Wisely, Hermocrates decided to keep his shocked and demoralized hoplites behind the city walls. The Athenians were undeterred, and in fact encouraged by the refusal of their enemy to meet them in the field. Now they busily started on the next stage of the siege.

In later ages siege warfare was a more dramatic business. But as the Spartans had shown earlier with their inability to take even little Plataea let alone the Long Walls between Athens and the Piraeus, fifth-century siege warfare gave a huge advantage to the defenders. With storming city walls being beyond contemporary technology, besiegers tended to concentrate on cutting off the enemy's food supplies and waiting for starvation to force a surrender. In this regard, the very size of Syracuse was a disadvantage for the defenders, because the large population meant that the people would starve all the faster. Of course, the larger the city, the longer the enclosing walls the besiegers would have to build. But Syracuse was more than half enclosed by the sea in any case, and the Athenians also now had Epipolae.

The Athenians started throwing a wall across the space that remained, across fields, marshes and broken ground alike, all with a speed and energy that left their opponents dismayed. Piles of building materials were dotted right along the planned course of the enclosure, and the Athenians were speedily joining the dots. It turned out (oddly enough for an army allegedly meant to help Egesta against Selinus) that the original expedition had conveniently brought along the masons, carpenters and other craftsmen needed to build just such an enclosing wall.

Construction had to be stopped or Syracuse was doomed. The Syracusans had little choice but to take the Athenians up on the offer of battle, which they had earlier declined. Yet, once both armies were drawn up outside the city, one look at the tight, professional ranks of the Athenians gave the Syracusan leaders pause. A second look at their own uneven levies, some still straggling into the field, led to the realization that the Syracusans were not offering battle – they were offering Athens the chance to perpetrate a massacre. With the cavalry providing cover, the Syracusan generals pulled their army back behind the walls unit-by-unit, leaving the horsemen outside to harass the wall-builders as soon as they recommenced work.

However, the Athenians now had cavalry of their own, albeit only a small force of some 650 horsemen. These were backed by infantry, and just as the Persians at Marathon, the Syracusans fatally underestimated how fast Athenian hoplites could move when they really wanted to. A mixed force of cavalry and hoplites caught the Syracusan horse flat-footed and gave it so severe a mauling that the cavalry too were driven back into the city, leaving the Athenians free to get on with their work. The enclosing wall was made of whatever was available, including stones from dismembered farm buildings and wood from what had once been the orchards alongside. The siege wall was intended to stretch from the sea just north of the river Anapus near the site of the first battle then up and over Epipolae, and to finish by bisecting the Catana road on the north shore at a point called Trogilus. Within days of the first failed attempt to stop it, the wall had already crossed the difficult marshes near the sea, and cut the Syracusans off from the river Anapus.

This enclosure left a small but significant Syracusan redoubt in the Olympieum. The Athenians had been given several opportunities to capture this temple enclosure, but the pious Nicias had declined to do so because he felt that the inevitable plunder of the temple's treasures would bring the wrath of the gods upon the expedition and – more prosaically – harm relations with Sicilian cities that Nicias still hoped to court. The Syracusans took advantage of Nicias's scruples and garrisoned the Olympieum with a mixed force of cavalry and irregular infantry, which were to be a thorn in the side of the Athenians thereafter.

The Syracusan leaders knew as much about military theory as the next group of Greek aristocrats, for all that they were somewhat ham-fisted at the practice. They knew that the way to stop the building of an encircling wall (known as a circumvallation) was to build a counter-wall at right angles across the path of the original. This cross wall provided a rampart that could be defended against the builders of the circumvallation. If this rampart could not be taken by the besiegers, the circumvallation would be forced to balloon outward to accommodate the cross wall within its enclosure.

The point at which the circumvallation could best be interrupted was decided to be an area near the temple of Apollo where the southern cliffs made it harder for the Athenians to get around to attack the back of the cross wall, which the Syracusans reinforced with palisades and wooden towers. To get the wall constructed fast enough to cut across the circumvallation before the Athenians closed the gap meant using whatever building materials could be obtained in a hurry, including the sacred groves of trees from temples within the city walls. Given the severity of the Athenian threat, the Syracusans readily made this sacrifice.

The counter-wall was constructed successfully and now lay right across the projected line of the circumvallation. The Syracusans were pleased with their high-speed construction, though somewhat disturbed that the Athenians had pretty much ignored it while beavering on elsewhere with their own wall. Given that the counter-wall made the Athenian efforts redundant, the Syracusans had assumed that work on the circumvallation would be abandoned. After watching the Athenian construction crews at work for a while, the majority of the defenders went back to the city. They left a strong garrison on their counter-wall and were prepared to swarm out to its defence as soon as it was threatened.

Those who returned to the city rapidly discovered that the Athenians had not ignored them altogether. Athenian engineers had been at work locating the underground pipes that carried spring water into the city, and these had now been broken.

The loss of their piped water supply discombobulated the Syracusans, but it was more of a nasty inconvenience than a crippling blow. One of the reasons that Syracuse had been founded where it was still bubbled up on the former island of Ortygia, now connected to the mainland by its long causeway. The famous spring of Arethusa remains in Syracuse today, on a terrace near the waterfront. It is surrounded by pale walls and planted with papyrus rushes, a gift from Egypt some 200 years after the Athenian siege. The nymph who gave her name to the spring was the beautiful Arethusa, a friend of the hunter-goddess Artemis, and like Artemis a virgin determined to remain that way.

Arethusa lived near Elis in the western Peloponnese, and one day, sweaty from the hunt, she made the mistake of bathing nude in the river Alpheus. This river is Alph, the sacred river of Coleridge's geographically confused poem *Kublai Kahn*, and even in Greek times the river was home to a powerful god. Bewitched by the beauty of Arethusa, this god tried in vain to seduce her, and when words failed, the river god tried a more direct approach, as Greek gods were wont to do. Arethusa prayed to Artemis to save her from rape, and the goddess came to the rescue, whisking her off to Sicily and transforming her into the spring. Yet the river god was undeterred. He sent the Alpheus plunging underground, through caverns measureless to man, and beneath the sea to Sicily. There, the waters of the Alpheus mingled with the waters of Arethusa, and in this way the river god slaked his passion. This was known to the Athenians, for it was famous that if a cup were dropped into the Alpheus in Greece it would eventually well up in the spring of Arethusa. One spring, however famous, would be hard pushed to supply all of Syracuse through a dry summer, even apart from the inconvenience of commuting to Ortygia to get it, which was exactly why the underground water pipes had been laid in the first place. It was another blow to undermine Syracusan morale, which was beginning to sag under an unrelieved series of setbacks.

And the Athenians were just getting started. Their opponents lacked the hard edge of an army that had been fighting the Spartans for the past decade or two and were still decidedly amateurish in their approach to warfare. For example, they liked a quick siesta after lunch, and some of the stockade guard even wandered back to the city to enjoy a post-prandial nap in their own beds. Those remaining kept a lackadaisical guard, since the Athenians had shown no interest in them as yet, and the fortifications they had erected were strong enough to repel any surprise attack.

Even having their cavalry charged by Athenian infantry had not convinced the Syracusans of how fast an Athenian hoplite in a hurry could move. Now the Syracusans received a practical demonstration as 300 hoplites burst from the Athenian lines and charged the stockade gates at a dead run. In fact, even Athenian hoplites could not move quite that fast, so the Athenians had taken the fleetest of their light infantry and given them extra armour for the occasion. These had only to hold the gate until regular infantry arrived moments later, and still well ahead of the bemused stockade garrison. Most of these were still unaware that their defences had been turned until they saw the entire Athenian army boil into furious action.

Half the Athenian army headed directly for the city gates in order to forestall any Syracusan reinforcements, and the rest flowed swiftly towards the counter-wall. The defenders of the counter-wall rushed to man the ramparts and discovered to their distress that the ramparts were already manned – by Athenians. Now it was the turn of the Syracusan garrison to show how fast they could move as they abandoned the wall and bolted for the security of the temple of Apollo.

It was a close race. As was usual with Greek temples, the building was surrounded by a sacred area – the *tenemos* – which was in turn surrounded by a wall. Syracusans and Athenians spilled into the *tenemos* together, but the

Athenians had been running a lot further and were more tired. Anyway, their immediate objective was not to annihilate the garrison, but to drive it off the counter-wall. In this they had succeeded, and the counter-wall was even now melting away as the triumphant Athenians gratefully mined it for building materials. Soon all that remained was a trophy of Syracusan armour mounted on a cross pole to show where the city's defenders had been chased from the field.

The Athenians put the Syracusan discomfiture to good use and started using their captured building materials to push their wall right across the marsh at the base of Epipolae, aiming to cut off Syracuse at the base of the Great Harbour. The successful completion of this stretch of the circumvallation would compromise the defences of the harbour to the point where the main Athenian fleet could be moved around the headland of Syracuse to support the troops directly. There was nothing for it but Syracuse had to start work on another counter-wall, presumably with the intention of this time providing it with a suitably chastised and alert garrison. This time they ran a ditch alongside the wall, both as an extra disincentive to fleet-footed Athenian attackers and also to slightly drain the boggy ground on which their wall was constructed.

Nemesis gets to work

Though the Syracusans still underestimated the energy and ingenuity of the Athenians, this cross-wall marked the turning point of their so far unrelieved series of defeats and disappointments. The shift in fortune certainly had little to do with Syracusan martial prowess, but a superstitious man might have felt the favour of the gods slipping away from the Athenians. Centuries later, the biographer Plutarch mused:

> Euripides, writing their funeral elegy, said that – 'Eight victories over Syracuse the Athenians gained, Heroes while the favour of the gods was equal to both.'
>
> And in truth there were not merely eight, but many more victories won by these men against the Syracusans. But the fact is that the gods intervened. Or was it Nemesis who halted the Athenians on their march to the pinnacle of power and greatness?
>
> Plutarch, Life of Nicias 17

Nicias fell ill, most probably with a kidney infection. Lamachus fell in battle. It happened early one foggy morning, just as Athens seemed on course for yet another minor yet convincing victory. Nicias had been unwell for some time, yet had forced himself to lead his troops. Now, finally, his constitution gave way, and he collapsed and was taken to the largest fort on Epipolae, which the Athenians called 'The Circle'. Lamachus led the army that day in an assault on the latest Syracusan cross-wall.

This was a combined operation, in which the fleet sailed from Thapsus, and appeared within the Great Harbour, just as the Syracusan garrison was thinking about breakfast. It looked as though the Athenians were planning on storming the beaches and taking the cross-wall from there. So the defenders rushed to defend against this huge raid from the sea. But the ships were empty of hoplites. While the enemy was distracted by the navy, the Athenian army swarmed down from Epipolae behind them and rushed at the ditch side of the cross-wall. In the van of the onrushing Athenians were the speedy 300, who flung themselves at the ditch with planks and doors looted from farm buildings. The main body of the army hardly broke stride as it swarmed over these makeshift bridges. Thereafter the Athenians were on the cross-wall before most Syracusans had figured out that they were not on the ships.

The more-or-less customary rout ensued. From the Syracusan point of view, getting beaten regularly meant that they were at least well-prepared for it, and cavalry were already galloping from the city to cover the retreat of their defeated soldiers. The garrison of the cross-wall were split into three groups. One group stubbornly held out on the wall itself (the Athenians mopped up this bit later) and another group bolted for the city. A third group found that they were already cut off by the speed of the Athenian assault. Instead they fled for the river Anapus and the same temple that had afforded shelter for the survivors of the Athenian capture of the first cross-wall.

Lamachus saw the opportunity of heading this group off at the bridge[40] and sent the fleet-footed 300 in hot pursuit. Running infantry in loose order make a perfect target for cavalry, and the Athenian runners saw the danger too late. They were hit by the horsemen before they could dress ranks. It will be remembered that some of the runners were skirmishers by profession, although they had been issued with heavier armour for their current duties. Therefore they were clumsy and inexperienced in forming a battle line, and as soon as the fleeing Syracusans saw their difficulties, they ceased their flight and joined in the cavalry attack.

Seeing a small part of his army in rout, Lamachus hastened to the scene, accompanied by some Argive volunteers and a few archers. In his haste to reach the troops in difficulty, Lamachus lost touch with the rest of his army.

After crossing a ditch, he and the half-dozen-or-so men with him attracted the attention of a group of Syracusan horsemen. Lamachus reacted in his usual heroic style by taking on the leader of the enemy group. This was one Callicrates, described by Plutarch as 'a man of high courage and a skilled warrior'.[41]

Lamachus himself was a fearsome fighter, so the duel had a positively Homeric character. It also ended with high tragedy. Lamachus slew his man, but was himself fatally wounded. He died in the field, and the Syracusans captured his body and armour.

Decapitated of leaders, the Athenian army briefly lost momentum. Their plan had worked perfectly. The Syracusans had been misdirected, defeated and routed. Now the hoplites wanted to know what to do next, and with Nicias incapacitated, Lamachus dead and Alcibiades long gone, the army was temporarily out of generals to tell them.

Seeing an unaccustomed uncertainty in their usually speedy and decisive enemy, other routing Syracusans turned to form a rough battle line. Someone on the Syracusan side was thinking clearly, for he reasoned that if the entire Athenian army was deployed alongside the Great Harbour on the ground between the marsh and southern city walls, then there was no one looking after Epipolae. This was a perfect chance to not only take the heights, but also to destroy the Athenian camp and stores.

Nicias was on his sickbed when his panicked servants informed him that a strong contingent of Syracusans were making straight for the fort. Fortunately, the Syracusans halted long enough to destroy almost 1,000 feet of the circumvallation, and while they were at it Nicias had a chance to review his options for defence. He had a line of siege engines outside the walls, standing amid huge piles of lumber intended for more walls and siege engines, and he had … nothing else apart from a handful of servants and kidney medication. It was not very much with which to throw back a substantial proportion of the entire Syracusan army, but as he had already demonstrated, Nicias was a resourceful man when he had to be.

As the Syracusans advanced on the fort, they saw servants running from pile to pile of lumber rapidly followed by smoke and flame. Even the siege engines were fired, as Nicias reckoned they were more easily replaced than the fort, the stores or himself. The Syracusans were taken aback by this development. The heights of Epipolae afforded a splendid view of events on the plain below to anyone who cared to look over his shoulder. Such a glance would have shown that after a spirited fight the rest of the Syracusan army on the plain was about done. The Athenian fleet was manoeuvring close to shore, and even though there were no soldiers on board, no one was keen on being hit from behind by several thousand sailors, especially as the Athenian hoplites looked like prevailing anyway. The Syracusan army decided to retire once again behind the city walls.

This did not leave a lot of time for the men on the hill, as their presence had now been noted by an Athenian army, which seemed frighteningly keen to do something about it. And tempting as the fort and the stores were, the only way to get to them was now blocked by a near-solid sheet of flame. The Syracusans were later to share their city with the great Archimedes. Now they showed some of that mathematical ability by subtracting the burn rate of the lumber from the attack speed of the Athenian army. The end figure was discouraging. Unless they got off Epipolae and back to their city at high speed, the Syracusans would be caught against the rock of a deeply annoyed Athenian army and the hard, hot place of a sheet of flaming siege materiel. The Syracusans withdrew, conceding the day to the Athenians and Nicias.

The Athenians put up a trophy to their victory, and in exchange for the body of Lamachus, they allowed the Syracusans to retrieve their dead. However, they did not cease work on the siege wall. Within days of the death of Lamachus, it seemed as if Syracuse would be hemmed in by a double wall on the land and by the Athenian fleet prowling off the shore. It now dawned on the Syracusans how completely they had underestimated the ingenuity, skill and determination of their enemy. Some began to talk openly of surrender.

Chapter 7

A Little Local Difficulty

I don't understand these long Athenian speeches. Why do they spend so much time praising themselves if they are not going to deny their aggression against our allies?

Stethelaides, euphor of Sparta, Thuc. 1.86

Gylippus

So discouraging was the news from Syracuse that it affected the plans of the force coming to the city's rescue. This rescue force was in any case somewhat less than imposing. It consisted of two Spartan and two Corinthian ships, or about three per cent of the number of better-built and more capably manned Athenian ships currently making themselves at home in Syracuse's Great Harbour. Nicias, who was now in sole command of the Athenian war effort in Sicily, dismissed the trickle of newcomers as opportunist privateers and decided that they were too few to have any effect on affairs in Sicily.

Aboard one of the Spartan ships was Gylippus, who was coming to the same conclusion. He was still at Leucas, the island that may once have been Ithaca, home of the legendary Odysseus (modern Lefkada), in the Ionian sea. Like Odysseus, Gylippus contemplated a voyage of uncertain prospects. According to the (erroneous) reports he had received, Syracuse was now fully enclosed by Athenian walls, and the city was on the verge of surrender. And as went Syracuse, so would go Sicily. Once the Athenians had demonstrated their ability to capture by far the largest and strongest city on the island, smaller cities would fall over themselves to make peace with Athens and get the best terms possible. There was always the example of Melos to encourage the obstinate.

So Gylippus, with typical Spartan pessimism, concluded that Sicily could be written off as a lost cause for the Spartan war effort. Instead, Gylippus decided to focus his energy on ensuring that at least Italy would not fall into Athenian hands. To this end he organized another twelve ships to follow his small flotilla, so that his diplomatic efforts might appear to be backed with at least a modicum of force. Then, having done all that was possible on the eastern shores of the Ionian Sea, Gylippus set course for Tarentum. This city being a Spartan foundation, Gylippus could at least be sure of a welcome there. He also had hope of Thurii, the city to which his scapegrace father had fled as an exile. As a child from that city, Gylippus could still claim citizenship there, and this he now did. However, even when he approached the city council as a returned native son, his appeals for support against Athens fell on deaf ears. Like the Sicilian cities, the Italian Greeks were shocked and awed by the vigour and skill of the attack on Syracuse and the almost unbroken string of Athenian successes that had followed.

Gylippus determined to press north towards Etruria and personally present his case to the cities there, a move that would take him far from the crucial cockpit of events in Sicily. But as Gylippus set off on his diplomatic mission, a strong seasonal north wind set in, blowing his ships out to sea. Getting back to the coast was difficult enough and going further north was out of the question. Gylippus returned to Tarentum, intending to refit his battered ships and to mull over his next course of action. At Tarentum he discovered that Syracuse was not in fact completely surrounded and nor had the Syracusans completely resigned themselves to surrender, though both events were expected to happen within a few weeks at most. This caused Gylippus to hastily revise his plans. Instead of sailing to north Italy, he would go south after all, and see what could be saved in Sicily. The Spartan general may even have taken a moment in his prayers to thank whatever deity was responsible for the fortuitous wind that had prevented what might otherwise have been a disastrous strategic move. And indeed, history was to show that the wind that brought Gylippus to the battlefront was the pivot on which the campaign turned.

Within Syracuse there was fear, uncertainty and doubt. The Syracusan army was led by aristocrats, as was generally the case with ancient armies everywhere. The completeness with which these generals had fallen into each and every trap the Athenians had set for them led some to doubt that mere incompetence could produce such a perfect score. Was there perhaps a secret deal by which the Athenians had agreed to hand the city over to oligarchic rule in exchange for some well-timed blunders? There were many who believed that this was so. These doubters forced the resignation of the generals in question and replaced them with known democratic sympathizers. Then, deciding that if the oligarchs in the city were already negotiating with Nicias, they might as well do the same, the democratic party sent heralds to discuss whether they could remain in power even if Syracuse surrendered.

Nicias was already reported to be receiving ambassadors from all over Sicily from cities that were hastily reconsidering their former neutrality. These ambassadors were often accompanied by shiploads of grain donated as proof of goodwill and sincerity.

> It was generally believed that Syracuse was as good as taken, and everyone tends to jump on a bandwagon ... There was a growing body of opinion that the Athenians were all-powerful and led by a general whose outstanding ability and fortune made him unbeatable.
>
> Plutarch, *Life of Nicias* 18

There remained only a small gap in the enclosing wall and piles of material had already been positioned across the gap they were to fill. The Syracusans had actually called an assembly to discuss the terms on which they might negotiate a surrender when a fast trireme from Corinth arrived under the city walls. This trireme had slipped through an Athenian security cordon perhaps made lax by the belief that it was all over bar the shouting, and its captain bore the news that help, in the form of Gylippus, was on the way.

Gylippus was well aware that the arrival of a single man would not greatly hearten the Syracusans. He needed to make the point that he was not merely Gylippus, but also the physical manifestation of Sparta, and the reputation of that city was worth a regiment. To make this point, Gylippus first took himself to Himera. This, the most westerly of the Greek cities on the north coast of the island, had two advantages. Firstly, it was right on the front line, where Greek repeatedly clashed with Carthaginian for mastery of Sicily. Gylippus could argue that if Syracuse were taken the Carthaginians would be emboldened to take Himera. Whatever the local disagreements, Syracuse had always defended Greek interests against Carthage. But, asked Gylippus, would this be the case if Syracuse was under new management and taking orders from people hundreds of miles across the sea who had completely different priorities?

Furthermore, Himera was close to the Athenian enemy of Selinus. With Syracuse disposed of, it was probable that a large Athenian host would duly arrive to sort out Selinus. Then, Athens being Athens, Himera would probably be sorted out at the same time so as to save the Athenians the inconvenience of coming back to do so later.

The Himerans may have been more reluctant to take the side of Syracuse but for another stroke of fortune. The Sicels in their part of the interior had been strongly pro-Athenian; less through their own inclination than because of the strong leadership of Archonidas, the local king and a firm friend of Athens. However, Archonidas had just passed away and his successor was uninterested in taking one side or the other. This meant that the Himeran hoplites would not be leaving their homes behind in hostile territory.

These happy circumstances allowed the Corinthian messenger who reached Syracuse to announce that Gylippus was not only on his way, but was backed by a substantial force. There were 700 sailors, some armed and prepared to also serve duty as soldiers, 1,000 regular foot from Selinus and Himera, over 100 cavalry, and light infantry that included not only Selinites but also 1,000 Sicel volunteers. The messenger and his ship were themselves the forerunners of a modest fleet on the way from Corinth, with the expectation that even more ships were to follow. There were also reports that Sparta – constantly urged on by Alcibiades – was becoming increasingly peeved with Athenian support for Argos and felt that the spirit of the peace treaty had long since been abandoned. The main architect of that peace was Nicias, and while he was away in Sicily he was unable to use his diplomatic contacts to soothe the exasperated Spartans.

In fact, it is quite possible that one of the main factors keeping the peace in Greece was actually the Athenian expedition to Sicily itself. If this succeeded and Athens conquered Sicily, Sparta might be forced to back down even in the face of repeated Athenian provocations. If the expedition failed disastrously, Sparta would happily join in finishing off a weakened Athens. Therefore, the famously cautious Spartans were keeping their options open until they discovered how Gylippus was faring.

Gylippus takes charge

The Spartan general and his scratch force from Himera arrived at the nick of time. Nicias was still unwell, and with Syracuse expected to surrender in any case, work on the wall had gone from frantic to dilatory. There remained two small incomplete sections, one of which was between the main Athenian fort and the sea, which meant that a sufficiently determined force might still be able to bull its way over Epipolae and into the city.

The inertia of the Athenians both now and hereafter cannot be explained simply by the belief that the war was all but won. Their laxity is almost startling in comparison to their earlier dynamism. Undoubtedly, the fact that Nicias was enfeebled by illness was a partial cause, but the aristocratic historians of the ancient world probably greatly underestimated the energy which the relatively low-born Lamachus brought to the campaign. With his death the initiative passed from the Athenians to the Syracusans. Though Nicias continued to manage affairs competently and scored further successes, the expedition's record after Lamachus slips from brilliant to mediocre at best.

Among the areas where the Athenian effort had fallen below par was intelligence gathering. Consequently, they had no idea what Gylippus had been up to, and his appearance on the north shore beside their fortifications took them completely by surprise. Despite this they quickly formed into battle array and prepared to repel the unwelcome intruder. But instead of fighting, the red-cloaked Spartan general sent a herald to announce that if the Athenians were prepared to quit Sicily, he would allow them five days' free passage.

The incredulous Athenians made no formal reply, but unofficially the hoplites mockingly pointed out that they had recently released from prison several hundred Spartans, every one of whom had once sported a redder cloak that Gylippus wore, and yes, their hair had been longer too.[42] Syracusans might be overawed by a representative from Sparta, but the Athenians had been fighting Sparta for decades, and until recently they had been getting the better of it. For them, the arrival of one Spartan changed nothing.

Seeing that their reinforcements had arrived, the Syracusan army emerged from the city and began gamely forming into battle order. Gylippus had until then been preparing his volunteers for a fight to break through the Athenian line opposing him, but after an appalled look at what the Syracusans considered a fully-dressed battle line he changed his mind. He decided it might be better to offer battle on more open ground and moved his army to where the inexperienced Syracusan levies could have a second crack at forming a battle line in easier circumstances.

Had the martial Lamachus been present, there is a good chance that the Athenians would have accepted the opportunity now offered and given battle. Being war-hardened veterans, they might well have won it too. But the cautious Nicias was now in sole charge, and he had been given a bad scare in the previous engagement, which had seen Lamachus killed and Nicias endangered. By his reasoning, the Athenians had a perfectly good defensive wall, and even with an annoying Spartan hovering about outside it, there was no reason for the Athenian army to go on the offensive. Let the enemy take on the Athenian fortifications, and after they had failed the Athenians would close the last gaps in their defensive wall. With Syracuse fully surrounded, the city would fall without the risks that a full-scale battle entailed.

The strategy was perfectly logical and very unAthenian. Where before the Athenians had been pro-active, inventive and aggressive, under Nicias they were cautious, defensive and not so much prepared to surrender the initiative as to actively force the opposition to take it. Undoubtedly, both Syracusan and Athenian hoplites recognized the change in mood, and the morale of the two armies shifted accordingly.

When the Athenians refused battle Gylippus led his army to a secure spot on high ground and camped there for the night. The next day, the Athenians were still waiting passively behind their walls, so Gylippus blooded his men by leading them in an attack on one of the minor Athenian forts on Epipolae. This he captured handily, and put the defenders to death. From surviving accounts of the action that followed, it is uncertain whether the capture of the Athenian fort allowed Gylippus to link his forces with the Syracusans, or whether the one force continued to operate from the city while Gylippus kept his little army on the other side of the Athenian lines.

Meanwhile, encouraged by Athenian inactivity, Syracusan ships made a snap raid from the docks and captured an Athenian ship incautiously moored nearby. The same people who had been gloomily contemplating inevitable surrender a few days ago were now feeling almost as energetic as the Athenians had previously been. Undeterred by their two previous failures, they now decided to throw out yet another cross-wall. This latest attempt was to run from Achradina up Epipolae, towards where Gylippus was encamped.

This was also probably the last point where the Athenian fortifications were either weak or incomplete, for the methodical Nicias had completed the circumvallation of the land near the harbour before moving his forces to the heights. Nicias was all the more eager to complete the fortifications on the lower ground because about a third of the Syracusan cavalry was stationed at the Olympieum, near the site where the Athenians had first landed and fought their first battle. The completion of the circumvallation at this point meant that the cavalry were now effectively behind the Athenian lines and cut off from the city.

The Athenians now distributed their forces along the wall, each section guarded by a different group of the allies they had recruited into the invasion. The weaker sections they guarded themselves, as Gylippus discovered when he led a night attack against a flimsy-looking section of wall. While the wall might have been weak, there was nothing feeble about the well-armed and ferocious veterans who defended it, and Gylippus hastily pulled back his motley force before it came to serious harm.

With Syracusan cavalry roaming Epipolae in front of the Athenian fortifications and the cavalry from Olympieum active behind the Athenian lines near the harbour, communications between the different parts of the besieging force increasingly went by sea. Therefore Nicias decided it was time to move the fleet to the Great Harbour itself. Since the mouth of the harbour was guarded by Syracusan-held Ortygia on the north side, Nicias helped himself to the south side, on a headland called Plemmyrium, which faced Ortygia across three-quarters of a mile of water. On Plemmyrium Nicias constructed a series of forts and rudimentary docking facilities. There were three main forts that were used as depots for the equipment of the sailors and their ships, but the site was far from ideal.

For a start, there was little fresh water, and the Syracusan cavalry from the Olympieum at large outside the enclosing Athenian wall made gathering fuel or supplies a risky and occasionally fatal business. Furthermore, the lack of any sophisticated harbour facilities made maintaining the ships more difficult. This was important, for ancient warships needed a substantial amount of maintenance to remain in peak condition, and the Athenian ships had been operational for two summers. Thus Plemmyrium was a tough posting for ships and crews alike, and all the while the fleet was at this station its battle-readiness steadily deteriorated.

As was often the case with sieges, more fighting was done with saws and shovels than with the sword. Gylippus had joined in the work on the Syracusan cross-wall. His capture of the small fort had gained him access to Athenian building materials for the circumvallation, and now the chagrined Athenians saw these same building materials being incorporated into the cross-wall.

If he had not done so earlier, Gylippus had now joined forces with the Syracusans. Plutarch draws on contemporary historians[43] to report that the Syracusans had mixed feelings about this. Some objected to handing command of their military affairs to this roughly spoken, long-haired stranger. By one report, the Syracusan generals accepted Gylippus as only an advisor, and even then over-ruled his advice. From the Spartan's point of view, this was intolerable. Given the past performance of the Syracusan high command, success was improbable unless they were replaced by a single – and vastly more competent – general.

The cross-wall had now reached almost to the Athenian circumvallation, so now the next item on the Syracusan agenda was to actually push past the

Athenian defences and drive that cross-wall westwards across Epipolae. This would effectively create a new district of the city between the cross-wall and the north shore. Such an extension would make the rest of the Athenian circumvallation redundant, for even if it were possible to stretch the surrounding wall to take in the area cut off by the cross-wall, the Athenians simply did not have the troops to effectively man such a huge stretch of fortifications. So if the cross-wall on Epipolae could break the circumvallation, the Syracusans would have taken a huge step in freeing themselves from the threat of Athenian conquest.

The first attempt was an ignoble failure. The Syracusans lost in part because they engaged the Athenians so closely that they were hemmed in by the fortifications and could not deploy the cavalry, which was always their most effective weapon. It was also suggested by some cynical souls that the Athenians had been tipped off about what to expect. The source of the tip was allegedly Gylippus himself.

Afterwards, while the Athenians were putting up their customary victory trophy and a herald was dispatched on his usual mission to ask permission for the Syracusans to gather their dead, Gylippus addressed the troops. He told them that there was nothing wrong with their fighting ability – they had simply been poorly-led into a bad position. Syracuse had the men and the resources to beat the Athenians. After all, the Syracusans were, like himself, Dorian. And it would be a total disgrace if Dorians should prove unable to overcome mere Ionians on the battlefield. Tomorrow the army would try again, Gylippus promised, and this time he would show them how to do it properly.

The Syracusan cross-wall and the Athenian circumvallation had now almost met to form a right-angle midway across Epipolae. It was clear that the battle of the walls would be won by whichever side could push their building project further, by just 100 yards or so. But for the battle on the next day, the Syracusans ignored the walls and formed up on that part of the high ground where neither cross-wall nor circumvallation had yet reached. There they waited until the Athenians, made confident by victory, advanced towards them.

The Athenians had further to go this time, as Gylippus deliberately held his army back and gave his javelineers plenty of practice on the Athenian line. It is probable that these javelineers were ordered to make their way around the right (south-eastern) flank of the advancing Athenian hoplites. Here, the lightly armoured skirmishers had the cross-wall nearer at hand for shelter if the Athenians rushed at their tormentors. And the torment was certainly effective, for on the right the huge hoplite shields carried on the left arm offered less protection, and virtually none after the javelineers had worked their way right around the flank. The skirmishers focused Athenian attention on the missiles raining down on them from the right. Yet this was not where the true danger lay.

The left (north-western) flank was unsecured, and while the Athenians were distracted by the javelineers, the Syracusan cavalry came thundering up and hit the exposed flank with devastating force. Under pressure from left and right, the centre could not hold. For the first time, the Syracusans were treated to the joyful sight of Athenian backs as the invading hoplites turned and fled to the safety of their fortifications. Gylippus had been proven right. With the right leadership the Syracusans could indeed beat the Athenians in a stand-up fight. As Plutarch remarked, 'Gylippus showed what a great thing experience is.' Now that Syracuse had a skilled general in command, the Athenians were going to find it much harder to get their own way.

Gylippus did not follow up far with his infantry. He had no wish to repeat the previous day's fiasco under the fortifications, and he had other plans as to how to use his victorious troops. So essential was this stage that although the army had just fought a minor battle, Gylippus kept his soldiers working through the night. The Syracusans were compensated for the loss of a night's sleep by the gain of a huge strategic success. The dawn saw the cross-wall stretching further across Epipolae than any possible Athenian attempt to contain it.

The completion of the cross-wall marked a highly significant point in the struggle. The breaking of the circumvallation meant that the Syracusans might yet be defeated in battle, but as long as they could hold the cross-wall there was no possibility that they would be starved into submission. In effect, the land campaign was effectively over, and the outcome of the campaign at Syracuse would be determined by events in the waters of the harbour.

A letter from Nicias

At this critical turning point in the campaign, Thucydides offers what purports to be an actual report on the current state of play written by none other than Nicias himself. This would not be the first account we have that is written personally by one of the protagonists in the Peloponnesian War, as Thucydides was himself an Athenian general. Nevertheless, a personal communication from Nicias would certainly add a first-person perspective to events, so historians have mused how genuine this missive may be. Certainly, a letter was written, and was read to the assembly by the city clerk.

It is also quite possible that the letter was archived and Thucydides saw this letter, or a copy of it. Regrettably, it is also possible that, despite the avowal of Thucydides that he always used as nearly as possible the words of the original protagonists in their speeches, the great historian may have been unable to resist adding a few rhetorical flourishes of his own. The letter reads:

Athenians,
   You have received many other letters in the past that have updated you on what we have been doing. Now it is essential that you become aware of current events and decide what is to be done about them. We were sent out against the Syracusans, and generally proved ourselves superior to them in battle. We built the fortifications that we now occupy. Now the Spartan Gylippus has arrived with an army raised partly in the Peloponnese and partly from the cities of Sicily. We beat him in the first battle, but the following day we were overwhelmed by the superior number of his javelineers and cavalry and we were pushed back into our fortifications. We are now pinned down by the enemy's greater numbers and cannot complete our circumvallation.
   The enemy's cross-wall has been pushed past the circumvallation, and we have no chance of blockading them unless we capture it. In fact their cavalry makes it hard for us to get far from our fortifications, so at the moment we are closer to being under siege than we are to besieging anybody.

Having pointed out that the situation on land was bad, Nicias hastened to assure his listeners that the situation at sea was desperate.

We originally had a first-class fleet, with excellent ships and superb sailors. Now the ships have timbers rotted from being so long in the water, and the crews have lost their form. We can't careen our ships, because the enemy has many ships of their own, and we would certainly be attacked if we took ours ashore for drying and cleaning. They [the Syracusans] don't have that problem, because they are not trying to block the harbour. They can beach their ships for maintenance whenever they like. They have the initiative, and use it to practice battle tactics at sea.

In conclusion:

As far as the expedition has gone, there is nothing for which you can blame the soldiers or generals. However, the whole of Sicily is united against us, and while we can hardly cope with what we are facing, another army is expected from the Peloponnese. Either the expedition should be recalled, or Athens must send yet another army as large as the first, accompanied by plenty of money. And I need to be replaced. While I was fit I gave excellent service, but now my kidneys are diseased and I cannot go on.

The letter is vintage Nicias. Wild optimism, a spirit of daring and willingness to improvise, the readiness to gamble and hold on to the initiative at all costs are features predictably missing from his communications, while his talent for accentuating the negative and an unerring ability to spot the cloud around every silver lining are prominently on display. One could sum up his situation report as 'every day, in every way, things are getting worse and worse'.

The not-very-fleet fleet
Athenians expected any communication from Nicias to be a litany of gloom, and his suggestion that the expedition was a bad idea that should be reversed at the earliest opportunity was hardly news. Therefore the Athenians cheerfully discounted Nicias's prognosis of doom. There was some reason to do so. Sicily was far from being as united against the Athenians as Nicias claimed, and in fact no army from the Peloponnese would be coming to rescue the Syracusans. The Athenians were tough, veteran troops, and despite the recent setback, their hoplites were more than a match for the Syracusans in battle. It is probable that the Athenians were aware of this, and dismissed much of what Nicias had to say as hyperbole intended to get him home as soon as possible. This was unfortunate, because Nicias was completely correct on one point. The fleet that the Athenians were soon to depend on for victory was indeed going to hell in a hand-basket.

Athenian triremes were regarded as female and sported names such as *Andrea* (Courage), *Aktis* (Sunbeam) and, in one delightful case, *Tryphousa* (Fusspot). And triremes were fussy. They could not sail in rough seas because they would broach if caught sideways by a large wave, and there was a constant danger of water entering through the oar ports. Constant exposure to salt water rotted ropes, oars and rudders, which needed frequent replacement, just as sails required constant maintenance. The ships had a very shallow draught and keel, which meant that a trireme could operate in very shallow water, but they could also capsize into that water with very little provocation.

More importantly, triremes were designed to be hauled regularly ashore for servicing. Because of this, it is believed that they were constructed of light wood, such as pine, which made it easy for the 170-man crew to beach it. However, the soft wood of these ships was not impervious to long-term exposure to water, and if they stayed too long afloat the hulls began to rot. Additionally, the whole ship was literally pulled together by two long cables (called *hypozomata*). These cables were kept taut while the ship was at sea, and this prevented joints from flexing and becoming fatigued. However, the cables themselves needed to be relaxed on occasion to prevent stretching, and this could not be done while the ships were on the water.[44]

A well-maintained trireme under sail and oar was one of the most beautiful sights the Mediterranean had to offer, and these sleek and deadly warships were the foundation of Athenian power in her island empire. However, such power came at a cost. Though a well-maintained trireme was good for a quarter-century or so, Athens usually had a fleet of some 300 ships, and needed to build at least twenty-five a year to replace ships taken out of commission for one reason or another. Though the ships were built to a standard model from prefabricated parts, this still absorbed a large amount of money and manpower, and this was before the considerable amount of maintenance was taken into account.

The triremes of the Athenian expedition had completed an unknown amount of service beforehand and then made the journey to Sicily itself, and this was no short trip for an ancient warship. Then they had passed a winter in sub-standard quarters and two summers on the water, while receiving little more than essential maintenance. The hulls were becoming encrusted with marine life and were taking in water, and sails were becoming ragged, as was discipline among the crews.

Greek warships were powered by free men, and consequently a Trierarch had only limited powers over his crew. It did not help that the population of Athens and other states fell constantly short of the number of rowers every maritime Greek state required, and it is a fair bet that a proportion of the rowers on the expedition were mercenaries. Some of these would not have expected to be retained for so long, and others resented the harsh conditions of life at Plemmyrium. Some men actually opted out of service and gave their captains slaves in their place, falsely asserting that the replacements could row every bit as well as they could.

Added to fraying discipline and the tensions to be found when any large body of men are confined in uncomfortable conditions for a considerable time, there were the added discomforts of poor supplies and water thanks to the interdictions of the Syracusan cavalry, and the threat to health that this posed.

In short, both in terms of ships and crews, the fleet was a sorry shadow of the brave ships that had raced so merrily from the harbour of Piraeus two summers ago. The same commanders who had once confidently driven the Syracusans from their harbour knew that it would no longer be so easy to keep them out. A time of reckoning was approaching, and both sailors and their general were gloomily aware that the fleet was likely to be found wanting.

A winter of preparations

The battle that prevented the Athenians from enclosing Syracuse with a circumvallation was the last major action of the year. Nicias now had high hopes of being relieved, and moderate hopes of the expedition being called off and rated as a losing draw for Athens. In neither eventuality did he see that there was much to be gained from offensive action, while there was yet plenty that could be lost. Therefore the Athenians stayed within their fortifications and made few attempts to gain ground, even on the diplomatic front. After all, there was no point in attempting to bring over allies whom Nicias hoped would have to be abandoned in spring anyway.

Around the midwinter solstice the Athenian assembly prepared a small fleet of ten ships for a tricky winter crossing to Sicily. This ship was to bear an unwelcome present to Nicias – the news that the expedition was not being withdrawn and he was not to be replaced. There would indeed be replacements, but for the fallen Lamachus and the absconded Alcibiades.

One general who would be joining Nicias was Eurymedon, a general named after the successful naval battle of the same name in the early 460s when a combined Greek fleet had beaten the Persians. This Eurymedon had been to Sicily twelve years earlier, as one of the leaders of the Athenian fleet that had been sent packing after the successful diplomacy of Hermocrates (pp.30–1). The Athenians had fined him heavily for his unsuccessful performance on that occasion and assumed that the painful experience would make him determined do better this time around. Eurymedon was to be accompanied by 120 talents of silver, which would let the men of the expedition know that they had not been forgotten at home.

Eurymedon informed the expedition that even now another replacement general,[45] Demosthenes – perhaps the best Athenian general remaining – was conducting a winter tour of the city's island empire, screwing as much cash and as many recruits as he could get from the ever more recalcitrant subjects of Athens. Having unloaded his cash cargo and the bad news for Nicias, Eurymedon did not remain in Sicily, but braved the winter waves yet again to join in organizing the massive reinforcements Athens would be sending.

In part, this cash was to be raised by an extra tax of five per cent on all imports and exports by sea. Though the measure was successful in raising revenues in the short term, the Athenians were also discovering the law of diminishing returns. The more they raised taxes, the more they discouraged all but the most profitable enterprises. Trade that was marginally profitable in the first place was simply abandoned. Economic activity declined, and the Athenian tax take dropped with it. Nevertheless, in the short term enough funds were raised to ensure that when Demosthenes did set off for Sicily in the spring, he would be accompanied by a formidable force. Unlike the ailing Nicias, the Athenians had by no means given up on their Sicilian project.

Some note was taken of Nicias' dire warnings. A fleet of some twenty-five ships was to be dispatched to the trading city of Naupactus on the northern shore of the Corinthian Gulf. From there this force could intercept and destroy any invasion fleet setting out from Corinth almost before the hoplites aboard were out of sight of their mother city.

In Sparta there was debate. The cold war with Athens was already lukewarm and there was a party (predictably led by Alcibiades) eager to heat things up to the next stage beyond that. As far as this group was concerned, the peace treaty with Athens had been tattered for some time, but was finally shredded beyond all redemption by the ever more blatant Athenian support for Argos, with which city the Spartans were still at war. The Athenians had never handed back Pylos, on the coast of Laconia, and from there they had launched a series of constant harassing raids into the Laconian interior. Indeed, that summer they had gone further and put together a fleet of thirty ships in support of Argos, and this had devastated several small Spartan towns. The Athenians had rejected every Spartan appeal to submit their differences to arbitration, so the Spartans concluded that enough was enough. Next spring would see war with Athens.

With this decided, the Spartans moved on to planning the course of that war. Firstly, they and their allies would prepare reinforcements to be sent to Syracuse. As Gylippus had shown, the value of Spartan reinforcements lay less in their numbers than in their quality. Every Spartan would fortify a Syracusan battle line that was already abundantly equipped with men and enthusiasm but lacking experience and staying power. Away from the battle line, the war-hardened Spartans would also help with the training and discipline that the Syracusans were currently so fatally lacking.

The next question was how to organize the annual summer hike to Attica. Every year, during the first phase of the war, the Spartans had marched to Attica and devastated the countryside, which had stubbornly bounced back into productivity once the Spartans had left. To date, the only effect, other than healthy exercise, had been for the army to leave Sparta itself exposed to attack since the Athenians could get there by sea considerably faster than the Spartans could march back over land.

Alcibiades had some ideas about that.

Chapter 8

The War Goes to Sea

> You are the first to stand up to the Athenians and that navy of theirs which has given them everything … When beating the champions you become champions yourselves.
>
> Gylippus to the Syracusan naval force, Thuc. 7.66

Decelea

As the spring arrived in the year 413 the Spartan plans became clear, and these were highly discomforting to the Athenians. At the urging of Alcibiades, the Spartans occupied and fortified the village of Decelea on a mountain pass between Thebes and Athens. This gave them a year-round presence in Attica, within sight of Athens itself. The arrival of Spartan troops on a semi-permanent basis caused those Athenian farmers contemplating sowing crops for the next year to wonder if the effort would be worth it. As fate would have it, some of the most fertile parts of Attica lay so close to Decelea that any attempts at farming the land there would be observed and permanently discouraged by the Spartan cavalry.

Agricultural issues aside, the Athenians had yet further cause to curse the renegade Alcibiades for his suggestion. Despite earlier Spartan incursions during the recent war, food supplies had been shipped to the island of Euboea and then overland to Athens. With the Spartans at Decelea poised to interdict such overland shipments, supplying the city was now much more difficult than it had been previously.

Another effect of the new Spartan fort was on the Athenian labour supply. In Attica, as in most of the ancient world, many demeaning, difficult or dangerous jobs were done by those who had no choice in the matter – that is, by slaves. At Decelea the Spartans offered shelter to any Athenian slaves who took refuge with them, causing many abused farm workers and domestic servants to leave their current employment without notice.

More importantly, the Spartans offered shelter to the slaves who laboured in wretched conditions in the mines of Laurion. The silver mines at Laurion were the main engine of Athenian wealth, and supplying the mines with manpower was one reason that the Athenians enthusiastically enslaved the populations of the cities they captured. Mining in the ancient world was a dangerous and unhealthy business. It required frequent resupplies of manpower to replace the short-lived unfortunates who worked in dank, overcrowded conditions where health and safety regulations were unheard of. Certainly, mining was not work that anyone undertook voluntarily.

Therefore as soon as word circulated among the slaves in the mines that Sparta was offering refuge to fugitives, every worker who had a chance slipped away and made the dangerous journey across Attica to Decelea. Thousands escaped. Thucydides estimates that the mines alone lost some 20,000 workers before the end of the war, apart from those who got away from the fields and households of Attica.[46] Most of those who escaped were skilled artisans, since these were necessarily given more freedom of movement that the wretches who did the actual digging, so not only did Athens lose manpower, but it lost the type of slave manpower it could least afford to lose.

It goes without saying that fortifying Decelea was an outright act of Spartan aggression tantamount to a declaration of war. The Spartans were quite comfortable with this. As far as they were concerned, the taking of Decelea was a mixture of retaliation and self-defence. Argos was now waging full-scale war on Sparta, and the Athenians had been aggressively supporting Argos. The Athenians had not merely broken the spirit of the peace, but also the actual terms, since Athenian raiding parties had struck deep into Laconia. The repeated Athenian provocations and refusal to negotiate had pushed the cautious Spartans into war. Perhaps the Athenians should have recalled it was a similar policy of unprovoked aggression which had initially got them into trouble with Persia. It is also quite possible that the Persians, who had long memories and were still technically at war with Athens and her allies, had by now started shipping funds to the Spartans as an incentive to resume the war. Certainly, Persia's envoys would have felt nothing but satisfaction on hearing of the Spartan fortification of Decelea.

The Spartans had for years been troubled by Athenian raids, and now the sandal was on the other foot. Athens was so close to Decelea that the Athenians henceforth had to keep a permanent guard on the city walls and have a standby force on hand in case the Spartans made a sudden foray against them. Athens was now on the front lines of the war its citizens had provoked, and the rest of Greece waited with interest to see how the city would react.

It was generally supposed that the Spartan presence in Attica would be the end of the war in Sicily. After all, what city would maintain a siege halfway across the Mediterranean when enemy soldiers were under its own walls? The Athenian force in Sicily had failed to gain any political traction over the winter, so new allies were few. On the other hand, the victory with which Gylippus had rounded off the previous year had gained Syracuse considerable support in both the Peloponnese and Sicily. Gylippus and Syracuse could expect to be reinforced as soon as the last storms of late winter relaxed their grip on the sea lanes of the Mediterranean. Since Nicias was barely hanging on against the foes he had now, any reinforcements would make his position untenable – especially as Athens could demonstrably use those soldiers in Attica.

And sure enough, as soon as the sea lanes opened, a force of almost 2,000 hoplites set off for the relief of Syracuse. Six hundred of these hoplites were from Sparta. They were not Spartiates, the top class of elite soldiers, but picked men from the helot and freedman class and formidable warriors nevertheless. They were escorted past Naupactus by twenty-five Corinthian warships; and the Corinthians in a rare burst of martial enthusiasm also contributed 500 hoplites of their own to the cause. In the event, these hoplites were late in getting started and only arrived late in the summer shortly before it was all over. The reinforcements were set to join with the forces that Gylippus was recruiting from the cities and hinterland of Sicily. Unlike the efforts of the Athenians on the island, the Spartan recruiting drive was meeting with enthusiasm and success. The tide of war was turning, and now it was Athens that seemed beleaguered by foes, just as Sparta had been a few short years before.

Naval action

Among those who espoused Spartan leadership of the Syracusan war effort was Hermocrates. He had apparently been among those generals whom Gylippus had displaced with his highly successful battle at the cross-wall the previous autumn; but if he had been deprived of command, Hermocrates nevertheless put the survival of his city above personal ambition and threw his political clout behind the Spartan general.

It will be remembered that Hermocrates had argued unsuccessfully for a bold effort to repel the Athenian invasion fleet at sea even before it landed in Sicily (p.52). His appeal had fallen on deaf ears, not least because the Athenians were renowned for their prowess at naval warfare. However, the Syracusans were now feeling cocky thanks to their one previous victory and the news that substantial help was on the way. They had beaten the Athenians on land, and if both Hermocrates and the skilled Spartan strategist Gylippus assured them that they could do so, they were ready to try beating the Athenians at sea.

As Hermocrates pointed out, the Athenians had habitually terrorized others with their daring and initiative, and for the last year the Syracusans had been on the receiving end of both. It was time to turn the tables. The Athenians felt secure in their mastery of the seas around Syracuse, and even a challenge to this supremacy would make a nasty psychological impact. A defeat would demoralize the Athenians yet more, even if hardly a ship was sunk. As was to be expected of the Athenian force since the loss of Alcibiades and Lamachus, the Athenians under Nicias might react with skill and vigour, but they would leave the initiative with the Syracusans. The first blow of the new campaigning season would be struck by Gylippus, and he intended to strike from an unexpected direction.

There were thirty-five Syracusan ships in the Great Harbour and another forty-five at the dockyards in the (Syracusan-controlled) Small Harbour. Athenian pickets were alerted by movement from both sets of ships in the early dawn light of a spring morning. The sentries hastily signalled the sailors at Plemmyrium to get the Athenian fleet into battle order as it rapidly became plain that the Syracusans intended to fight for mastery of the Great Harbour. To repel the Syracusans, the first objective of the Athenian fleet in the harbour was to prevent any more enemy vessels from getting in. Consequently, a fleet of sixty Athenian triremes raced for the entrance, with twenty-five ships peeling off from the main body to deal with the thirty-five Syracusan ships already present.

An ancient sea battle was a contest of oarsmanship and brute force. A trireme going into battle did so without sails, relying on the strength and stamina of the oarsmen. The initial phases of a battle might see organized flotillas advancing on the enemy in line, or curving through the water in an attempt to get around an exposed flank. Every trireme sported a wicked bronze-sheathed ram at the prow, tipped with three cutting blades for maximum penetration. It was a trierarch's dream to drive that ram amidships into an enemy vessel[47] and then back water as his opponent slowly buckled and sank beneath the waves. An alternative was to take one's ship at high speed alongside an unwary enemy trireme, snapping oars like breadsticks under the keel and causing chaos among the enemy rowers on the other side of those oars. This alternative was equally satisfying, because a ship thus treated was effectively dead in the water. A tight turn, and the ram could be used to dispatch the helpless victim.

In open water, a fleet action often turned into a sort of dogfight, with ships attempting manoeuvres on their own initiative, and the advantage going to the fleet that could best manage *ad hoc* collaborations between individual triremes. It was the sort of fighting at which the daring and inventive Athenians excelled. However, when ships stayed in close formation and manoeuvre was confined – for example by a harbour mouth – then an action at sea came closer to an infantry battle. The two lines of ships would end up jammed close against each other while the squads of marine hoplites (*epibatai*) aboard each ship punched it out, sometimes with impromptu interventions from the sailors if the enemy gained their decks. For the fight in the harbour, Gylippus had reckoned that the inexperienced Syracusans stood a far better chance at the latter type of battle, and he had arranged so that this is what came about.

The two lines of triremes were deadlocked. The Syracusans were unable to force their way into the harbour. In part this was because the practised Athenians carried more javelineers per trireme. Inexperienced men rushing about the deck of these narrow warships caused them to roll in the water, making life hard for the rowers. For this reason some Athenian javelineers cast their missiles while sitting down. The Syracusan ships held their own by sheer force of numbers. But if the Syracusans could not get in, their numerical superiority also made it hard for the Athenians to push them out.

As word of the battle spread through the city, spectators lined the walls of the Syracusan fortifications, and the Athenian soldiers in the forts at Plemmyrium came down to the beach to cheer on their sailors. This last was unfortunate, because Gylippus now launched his promised attack from an unexpected direction. He had taken a commando force out of the city in the dead of night and sneaked it around the Athenian lines. Then, while the Athenians were preoccupied with events at sea, he hurled this force at the landward side of the largest of the Athenian forts at Plemmyrium and captured it with hardly a javelin being thrown.

The stunned garrisons of the two smaller forts were suddenly presented with an invidious choice. Should they take on Gylippus's men in a race to gain their own fortifications, or take to the water and escape in the various merchant boats and support vessels on the beach before them? Even as some rushed to man the ramparts, less intrepid souls were taking option B, and it rapidly became apparent that those heading back to the ramparts were in an ever-shrinking minority. Eventually, the question became moot, since while the garrisons dithered on the beach the fast-moving Syracusans captured the forts. The waters of the harbour were the only remaining choice for the displaced Athenians. Even that option was complicated by the fact that the forward-thinking Gylippus had arranged for a fast-moving trireme to be cruising shark-like just offshore in expectation of just this outcome.

Hundreds of men and almost all of the Athenian naval supplies were captured. All that allowed many in the garrisons to escape was that the tide of battle in the harbour eventually turned in favour of the Athenians. The Syracusans fighting in the harbour mouth had eventually broken through – or alternatively, the Athenians had deliberately allowed them through, as they needed to rejoin their outnumbered comrades who were being beaten by the Syracusan ships already in the harbour. The Syracusans struggled into the Great Harbour in no sort of order, and once they were in open water the superior sailing skills of the Athenians came into play.

It has been estimated that a ship with waterlogged timbers was some fifteen percent slower than a freshly-tarred and caulked opponent.[48] On the other hand, those same waterlogged timbers caused the ship to weigh several tonnes more – an important factor when about a third of a trireme's weight was translated into kinetic force on ramming. And since Athenian seamanship more than made up for the speed deficit between the two fleets, a lot of ramming now happened, with the Syracusans on the receiving end. Ships that had triumphantly burst through the Athenian battle line minutes before suddenly found themselves totally outmanoeuvred and in frantic flight for the nearest safe beach.

With the attacking force routed, the entire Athenian fleet turned its baleful attention on the enemy ships already in the harbour. These ships had been doing pretty well against an inferior number of Athenians, but crumpled like wet parchment once the situation was reversed. In all, the Athenians captured the crew of three triremes. Those were the lucky ones. The infuriated Athenians butchered those aboard the other eight triremes that they captured, meaning that the Syracusan navy lost over 2,500 men and about ten percent of their fleet in the morning's action.

The Athenians had lost three ships, but they had also lost Plemmyrium. Without a naval base within the harbour the Athenian fleet no longer fully controlled the waters. Yet Nicias had moved most of the expeditionary force from Epipolae to the low ground alongside the harbour for the express purpose of being near the fleet. Now Athenian supply ships would have to risk attack from Syracusan triremes making a sudden dash from their base, or ambushers lurking by the harbour mouth. Furthermore, limited though they had been, the facilities at Plemmyrium allowed for at least limited servicing and maintenance of the ships. Now they had not even that. Thucydides' strategic summation makes no bones of how severe this loss was: 'This capture of Plemmyrium was first and foremost of the reasons for the deterioration of the Athenian army.'[49]

Also as Gylippus had predicted, the Athenians had been startled that they were challenged at sea in the first place. Then, despite the fact that they won a solid victory, the upshot of the morning's battle turned out to be that their strategic situation had markedly deteriorated. A feeling of aggrieved confusion took over the soldiers and sailors of the expedition, and this had a deleterious effect on morale.

War of attrition
Although they had denied the Athenians a base in the Great Harbour, the Syracusans were by no means secure once they ventured out from their own base. The Athenian fleet still held a grudge and soon after losing Plemmyrium the sailors made a spirited attempt to get at the Syracusan base. This was defended by the ancient equivalent of a minefield. A host of sharpened stakes had been driven into sand just offshore of where the Syracusan ships were at anchor. These stakes were carefully angled so that the points would drive through the hull of any oncoming ship, an arrangement that allowed security to the Syracusan triremes behind the wall of stakes even while they were on the water.

The Athenians brought up one of their largest ships and used this as a missile platform to suppress the fire of the Syracusan defenders while intrepid squads in small boats set about attaching ropes to the stakes and winching them out of the sand. The defenders in the dockyard took exception to this, but found it hard to argue with the Athenian ship that had been fitted with screens for archers to hide behind and towers to give javelineers greater range. When most of the visible stakes had been dealt with, the Athenians tracked down those that had been hammered in so deep that they were below the water line. Those found were sawn through at the base by divers. It was gruelling and dangerous work, and in the end not worth the effort. The Syracusans had practice at driving in the stakes and a goodly supply of replacements on hand. As soon as the Athenians had finished for the day, the Syracusans came out and replaced their damaged defences. Discouraged, the Athenians eventually abandoned their assault.

With their war at sea shaping up nicely, the Syracusans became bolder. A small fleet of twelve ships slipped past the Athenian blockade. One of these made the long voyage to Greece. It carried word that the defence of Syracuse was going well, and that the city's allies in Greece could help, both by sending more men and materiel and by making life uncomfortable in Attica by keeping troops at Decelea.

The other eleven Syracusan ships were on a search-and-destroy mission. Word had reached them that some Italian and Etruscan cities had prepared a supply convoy bringing stores to the Athenians. The Syracusan ships successfully intercepted the supply ships as they sailed south and destroyed both merchantmen and supplies. However, they were unable to prevent Etruscan soldiers making their way to Sicily, where they eventually joined with the Athenian army. After the action at sea, the Syracusan mini-fleet then went against the southern Italian tribe of the Locri, and there made a bonfire of timber stockpiled for the eventual reconditioning of the Athenian fleet.

That the Athenian ships needed reconditioning was made clear as the Syracusans made their way home along the east coast of Sicily. The Athenians were expecting them, and had prepared a welcoming party of some twenty ships. To their frustration, the lighter and smoother hulls on the Syracusan triremes allowed them to blow past the Athenian fleet, which barely managed to capture only the hindmost Syracusan vessel.

The capture of Plemmyrium had boosted the credibility of the Syracusan war effort. The ambassadors whom the city sent around Sicily with the news met with more receptive audiences than those they had encountered when Syracuse seemed on the verge of collapse. This new-found enthusiasm did not extend to the point of surrendering any warships to Syracusan control, but most cities agreed to contribute at least some infantry. Eventually, a force of around 2,300 men was raised, though the quality of the troops varied from city to city in both quality of training and type of equipment.

This show of solidarity among the Greek cities of Sicily was disturbing to Nicias, but equally disturbing to the Sicels of the interior. The tribesman had no illusions that unanimity among the Greeks of the island would be good for them if the Athenians were eventually driven from Sicily. Consequently, they listened readily to Nicias's suggestion, and prepared an ambush. The route of the reinforcing troops was easily divined, for little Akragas was still clinging stubbornly to the path of neutrality, and this left basically one route to Syracuse – that running via Leontini. A massive ambush was prepared and the execution met with partial success. Some 800 of the reinforcing troops were killed, but the remainder fought through to the walls of Syracuse. It was far from a conclusive victory, but it helped Athenian morale, not least because it reminded them that they still had Sicilian allies actively helping their cause. As a further boost to Athenian spirits, word came from Italy that pro-Athenian rebels had just won the southern city of Thurii in a coup, so the expected Athenian reinforcements would find a friendly staging-post on the Italian shore.

Fighting in the harbour

Despite the necessity of keeping at bay the Spartans at Decelea, the Athenians were still determined to send substantial reinforcements to Sicily. Raising these reinforcements had been no easy task – even wealthy Athens was feeling the financial strain of waging war on two fronts. The subject cities of the island empire were grudging in their contributions of men and money, for not only had the Athenians raised taxes yet again,[50] but now required a further levy of manpower for their expedition – and that before any of the men previously dispatched had returned home.

Nor, once he had put his reinforcements together, could Demosthenes set out hotfoot for Sicily. He had to go past Laconia on his way, and there take the time to demonstrate how much pain Decelea was causing Athens by setting up an equivalent on the Spartan shore. He fortified an isthmus as a base for raiding parties, and announced to the countryside that any defecting helots would find a welcome there. Then he set out for the island of Corcyra, the first stop on the way to Italy, picking up further detachments of troops along the way.[51]

At Naupactus the Athenian reinforcements were challenged by a Corinthian force stationed for just that purpose on the opposite shore to the pro-Athenian naval base. A hard-fought action ended in a draw, with three Corinthian ships lost and seven Athenian ships very badly damaged. Because the Athenians were considered as much masters of the sea as Spartan hoplites dominated warfare on land, the Corinthians claimed a victory because they had managed to hold their own in a sea fight. Nor did the Athenians deny this.

After patching and making good his battered ships, Demosthenes moved on to help his new Italian friends at Thurii. His leisurely approach to bringing vitally needed reinforcements to the Athenian siege effort at Syracuse may have seemed short-sighted, but Demosthenes was no fool. The siege of Syracuse was but the first stage in a long game intended to bring Greek Italy and Sicily into the Peloponnesian war on the Athenian side. There was no point in Athens winning Syracuse if Italy was lost in the process. As long as Nicias and his newly appointed colleagues Menander and Euthydemus did nothing rash, the siege of Syracuse could continue for a few more weeks without outside intervention.

It had also occurred to the Syracusans that it might be a good idea to persuade the Athenian generals to do something rash before Demosthenes got to them. Word of the naval action at Naupactus had reached Sicily, and the Syracusans were quick to learn how the Corinthians had managed to stand-off the vaunted Athenian fleet. It turned out that the Corinthian secret was a reinforced ram. Athenian rams were relatively light affairs, because the seamanship of the sailors enabled Athenian triremes to strike killing blows against the sides of enemy ships. Since they could not match this skill at manoeuvre, the Corinthians had modified their trireme design to make head-on collisions work in their favour. Thucydides describes the modifications with a sailor's enthusiasm.

> They cut the prows down to shorter and more solid versions, and packed reinforcing material into the sides by the cat-heads [cat-heads are the beams on either side of the prow]. The cat-heads themselves had stays of timber across them, going about 9 feet into the ship's side and projecting outward by about the same length.
>
> Thuc. 7.36

These solid rams would buckle the lighter, hollow rams of Athenian triremes in a head-on collision. The inability to hit an opponent in the side, which the Athenians considered a weakness, the Syracusans decided to turn into a strength. They would sail at the enemy in line abreast, and rely on the confines of their harbour to stop the Athenians from making any fancy flanking moves. In head-to-head collisions they would repeat the Corinthian success in severely damaging their Athenian opponents. Since the Athenians now held only a small portion of the harbour, a Syracusan ship in difficulty could put ashore almost anywhere, while an Athenian ship in the same situation risked capture.

Gylippus had garrisoned the largest Athenian fort but pulled the rest of the men who had captured Plemmyrium back to the Olympieum, where his cavalry and a number of irregular infantry were already based [p.86]. Now the Olympieum garrison marched out, apparently set on attacking a section of the Athenian siege wall. At the same moment Gylippus himself led out another set of troops from Syracuse itself and marched these towards the opposite side of the same wall. It seemed at first that the intention of the Syracusans was to attack the siege wall from both sides simultaneously – an action which, if it succeeded, would provide superior lines of communication between the Olympieum and Syracuse itself. The Athenian defenders quickly got into position to fight back-to-back against their attackers. Yet barely had the Athenian hoplites taken their place on the wall when the Syracusan fleet was sighted bearing down on them from across the harbour.

The Athenians uncharacteristically dithered. Some soldiers had responsibilities both on the wall and with the fleet, and were uncertain which should have priority. According to Plutarch, this indecision went right to the top of the Athenian force. The new commanders, Menander and Euthydemus, had not yet been in Sicily long enough for the pessimism of Nicias to wear down their characteristic Athenian gung-ho attitude. Like most Athenians, the new generals were by inclination pro-active, and they wanted an impressive victory to present to Demosthenes when he arrived. In vain Nicias argued that all Demosthenes wanted presented was a besieging force that was still intact when he got there. It was not in the nature of the new boys to refuse battle, especially when it was offered at sea. It became clear that the manoeuvres of Gylippus against the siege wall were little more than a diversion. The sea battle would be the priority, and Nicias was over-ruled by those who wanted to fight it. Consequently (and eventually) the Athenians manned seventy-five ships and sailed out to challenge a Syracusan fleet that slightly outnumbered them at about eighty vessels.

This was not the sort of freewheeling naval action at which the Athenians excelled. The only safe shore was a small stretch of land between the mouth of the river Anapus and the Lysimeleia marsh. Any ship that attempted to outflank the solid line of Syracusan ships risked being cut off from safety. Also the Syracusans made maximum use of the shores to ensure that at least one flank was generally tight against the land, so that the Athenians had little choice but to take on their armoured opponents head-on. As a further reminder that they were not fighting in open water, the Athenians were plagued by swarms of Syracusan special boat squadrons of skiffs and small, fast dinghies. Incapable of operating on the ocean, these little boats were totally at home in the harbour where they skirmished with the Athenian triremes, lobbing javelins into the tight-packed ranks of Athenian oarsmen and sometimes getting under the sweep of the oars to come alongside the hulls. In these latter cases, attacks on the oarsmen were probably ineffective, but would have upset the delicate co-ordination necessary to keep 200 men rowing in unison.

Despite these disadvantages, this was still the Athenian fleet. It might be powered by overworked rowers who were short of supplies and whose ships desperately needed a re-fit, but these were men who felt that mastery of the water was theirs by right, and they were not prepared to surrender it readily. The Syracusans too were somewhat tentative, as they had been roughly handled by the Athenians before. As a result, the day consisted of occasional tussles between ships uncertain of how to attack on the one side and afraid to press their advantage on the other. In the end both broke off the engagement without much having been achieved.

It fell to Nicias, the thoughtful pessimist, to work out what should be done if the Syracusans became confident enough to try to crush the Athenian fleet between their reinforced rams and the shore. He decided that the answer was to take a page out of the Syracusan book, and build a mini-harbour in a harbour. Not having a ready supply of sharpened stakes, he used merchantmen and other supply ships to create an artificial barrier behind which the Athenian triremes could fall if they were too hard-pressed. It was unlikely that the Syracusans would take time off from fighting the Athenian warships to deal with the merchantmen, but it was more probable that they might try to slip between them in pursuit of an Athenian trireme in difficulty. Nicias had an idea what to do about that too, and spent most of the next day getting things set up.

There had been some pondering going on on the Syracusan side as well. Rowing at battle speed took a lot out of the rowers, and by mutual consent both sides had broken off the previous battle at midday to allow their rowers to recharge with a quick lunch. A certain Ariston, generally considered to be the best steersman on the Syracusan side, came up with an idea to give his fleet a faster turn-around. Much of the earlier lunchbreak had been taken up by sailors heading back to the city to take lunch at home. This time Ariston prevailed on the city authorities to set up a provisions market right at the water's edge, and to make sure that many of the stalls were set up to supply the fastest food available.

So when battle recommenced after a day's break, the Athenians sallied forth from behind a line of merchantmen, while behind the Syracusan ships the first market stalls were appearing on the shoreline. The morning's battle was a repeat of the first round, with neither side prepared to commit to a decisive engagement. Then, as the day matured into afternoon, the Syracusans ships started to back water, and their ships gently reversed out of the battle. The Athenians decided that things were pretty much over for the day, and disembarked with food, trivial errands and a quick siesta in mind. They were astonished and indignant to discover that the Syracusan fleet had barely paused for its sailors to grab lunch on the go before returning to work.

Disorganized and resentful, the Athenian crews took their ships out to confront the Syracusans once more. Again, the Syracusans were disinclined to attack, but the Athenians were both annoyed and hungry. They were now prepared to force the kind of decisive action that they had avoided up until then. They threw themselves headlong at the Syracusan ships and discovered, as had their colleagues under Demosthenes, that the reinforced Syracusan rams really did work. According to the historian Diodorus Siculus,[52] not only had the Syracusans made their rams heavier, they had set them lower in the water, so that the Athenian ships rode up their opponents rams in a head-on collision. This caused their rams to hit below the reinforced cat's heads, while the Syracusan rams pierced them below the water-line.

There was a further advantage to the Syracusans in making their ships heavier and less manoeuvrable, and that was that they could carry more infantrymen. Had the Athenians caught these modified ships out at sea, they would have massacred them. But remarkably, it was the Athenians who were guilty of a failure of imagination, in that they still attempted to use ships and a style of combat suited to open water in the closed confines of the harbour. It is true that without a good naval base modifying their ships was harder, but there is no evidence that they even tried. So now, with their rams stove in and Syracusan marines raining javelins on them, the Athenians were at a decided disadvantage. It was their turn to back water and head for the safety of the beach. It was fortunate that Nicias had foreseen this possibility, for his barrier of stationary ships worked well. The fleeing triremes found safety behind the merchantmen.

Two Syracusan ships in hot pursuit came too close and discovered that the Athenian ships making up the barrier had strung 'dolphins' from loading cranes. These cranes usually operated from the docks, or were dismantled while a merchantman was at sea, since a ship with a crane assembled on deck was highly unstable. However, the merchantmen were securely anchored, and as the Syracusan warships hurried by intent on their prey they passed under the overhead beams on the merchantmen. A dolphin appears to have been a stake with a heavy pointed iron tip. The original ship-busting missile, this dropped from the beam and crashed through the deck below it and quite possibly through the hull as well. Certainly, the threat of these missiles stopped the pursuers of the Athenian fleet dead in their tracks, and the two unfortunates who were too late to avoid the dolphins themselves were simply stopped dead.

Nevertheless, a well-covered retreat could not hide the fact that the Athenians had been routed from the waters of the harbour and had lost another seven ships. Many more were badly damaged on a beach without dockyard facilities. There was no doubt that the Syracusans had convincingly won the battle of the harbour, and they put up a trophy to prove it.

For the Syracusans, this seemed the moment to push for a final victory. The Athenians had been driven from the water, and on land a now thoroughly dispirited Nicias had put his army into full turtle mode. The Athenians retreated within their fortifications, completely surrendered the initiative and did little more than fight off Syracusan probes on their defences. The clearing of the Athenians from Epipolae had been a possibility ever since the success of the cross-wall there had prevented the Athenians from completing their siege line on the hill. Now the Syracusans started considering this as their next project; a move which, if it were successful, would see the once-proud Athenian expeditionary force huddled against the marsh and surrounded by enemies.

The plan was to launch another combined forces operation of the type that had begun the battle of the harbour, though this time the telling blow would be struck by the infantry with the fleet in support. The plan was never put into execution. As the Syracusans prepared their attack, the hulls of seventy-three Athenian warships, escorts for a host of merchantmen and transports, appeared over the horizon. Demosthenes and the Athenian reinforcements had arrived.

The Syracusans had been expecting the expeditionary force to be reinforced, but knowing of the Athenian difficulties with the Spartan force at Decelea, they had expected the reinforcements to be an inferior scratch effort. The seventy-three triremes – a third of the total Athenian fleet – were the first hint of how wrong this expectation had been. The dismayed soldiers on the Syracusan ramparts watched as 5,000 hoplites disembarked from the transports. They were accompanied by a host of javelineers, archers and other light infantry, while the sailors turned their attention to unloading massive stores of war material and supplies from the merchantmen. It was clear that the Syracusans had underestimated the energy, commitment and resourcefulness of the Athenians. The defenders of the city who had come close to defeating the first wave of invaders and throwing them off the island now faced reinforcements almost as numerous and well-equipped as the original expedition had been. It looked as though the Syracusans were going to have to start all over again.

Chapter 9

The Final Phase

Everyone makes mistakes, but the man who sees this and changes his ways does well. It's the stubborn man who shows himself a fool.

Sophocles, *Antigone* l.1138

Demosthenes was a pretty good general. We first hear of him as a *strategos* in 426, when he assisted the Messanians of Naupactus in their campaign against the Aetolians. He overcame initial setbacks (Thucydides, who may have been a relative of Demosthenes, says the setbacks were because he trusted too much in the advice of his allies) and won a convincing victory, which consolidated Athenian power in an area crucial for sea passage to the west. It was Demosthenes who decided to fortify Pylos the following year while his fleet was en route to Corcyra; an action that led directly to the most convincing Spartan defeat of the war [p.16]. Demosthenes did not get any credit for his operation at Pylos, partly because the demagogic Cleon was determined to mop up any political benefit that was going, and partly because Demosthenes' use of missile troops and unconventional tactics was seen as demeaning traditional hoplite warfare. Even Thucydides preferred to assume that success on the part of Demosthenes was mainly due to good fortune.[53] Consequently, although he was the junior commander in a bungled Boeotian campaign, Demosthenes was made the scapegoat for its failure. He remained out of favour with the assembly until 413, when he was elected to bring reinforcements to Sicily.

Nicias remained the senior commander of the expedition, but he was in poor shape physically, and the recent series of setbacks had completely convinced him of the folly of an expedition he had never approved of in the first place. Nicias welcomed the energetic and decisive Demosthenes almost as much as the soldiery and was quite prepared to allow the newcomer to act as his *de facto* replacement. The arrival of Demosthenes and the massive reinforcements he had brought with him had so cowed the Syracusans that they had abandoned their plans for offensive action on Epipolae and taken up a defensive stance within their walls. The initiative had once more passed to the Athenians, and in Demosthenes they had a commander who had clear ideas of how to use it.

The first stage was to secure the land around the river Anapus and ensure clear lines of communication for the expeditionary force. This was done with despatch, despite some interference from the Syracusan cavalry and light infantry stationed at the Olympieum. This essential preliminary complete, Demosthenes turned his attention to what he considered the crux of the entire war in Sicily – Gylippus's cross-wall on Epipolae. Essentially, matters could be considered as follows. The purpose of the expedition was to secure the west for Athens. While Alcibiades might have brought the Greek cities of Sicily into a coalition similar to the Delian League, this was always unlikely, and without the political skills of Alcibiades none of the other Athenian generals even had a chance of managing it.

With diplomacy insufficient, this left a military solution – and the problem with a military solution was Syracuse. The preceding years had made plain that while Syracuse resisted, most Greek cities in Sicily would at best be neutral to Athens and at worst actively opposed. On the other hand, if Syracuse could be brought to heel, the rest of Sicily would soon follow, and Italy thereafter. Nicias had come close to realizing this objective. Even the threat of Syracuse being fully enclosed by a siege wall had nearly brought the city to terms. If that wall was now completed Syracuse would be denied further reinforcements and supplies. Therefore Gylippus's cross-wall not only lay across the proposed Athenian line of enclosure, but also across the entire master plan for subjugating the west. It had to go.

If the cross-wall stayed, the Athenians could not. By now it was early August and Demosthenes could clearly see that all the Athenians were currently achieving in their encampment by the marsh was wasting troops who could be usefully deployed in other theatres of war. It was time to force a decision. If the enclosure of Syracuse with a siege wall failed, then the expedition too was a failure. There would be nothing for the Athenians to do but cut their losses and leave.

This reasoning left Demosthenes with one course of action. The Athenians would throw their full strength at the cross-wall. If they took it, they would proceed with their siege wall, cut off Syracuse from help and supplies and force the city to terms. If the attack failed and the Syracusan cross-wall stayed, then the Athenians would go home. It was that simple.

Ill met by moonlight

While operations had been taking place around the harbour, the Syracusans had been working hard on that cross-wall. This had grown from a simple barricade in front of the Athenian enclosing wall to almost an extension of the Syracusan city walls right across Epipolae. The passage up the hill where the Athenians had originally gained possession of the high ground was back in Syracusan hands and guarded by a fort. By way of back-up if that fort should fall were three other smaller forts. Presumably as a guard against treachery, each fort was manned by a different group, one garrison being Syracusan, another of contingents of the Sicilian cities, and a third of other allies. Extensive outworks connected the various forts, and an emergency stand-by force of 600 Syracusans with experience of fighting on Epipolae made up a further reserve. Hermocrates had once failed to take Epipolae through carelessness and ineptitude. Gylippus did not intend to lose Epipolae in the same fashion.

After a thoughtful study of the problem, Demosthenes decided that his best chance of taking the hill was by a surprise attack. He had undoubtedly been informed of the unsporting Syracusan conduct in the harbour where the navy had fought during what should have been a lunchbreak, and he intended to take this behaviour a step further. So far there had been no major action at night – not only in Sicily, but throughout the entire Peloponnesian war. The Syracusans had no reason to expect one now, so this would give the Athenians the element of surprise so essential to the assault.

Demosthenes planned this assault carefully and made sure that the attacking troops took supplies for five days, so that even if the Syracusans re-took the passage leading to the heights his army could hold out until Nicias organized a relief effort.

On a clear night the Athenians moved stealthily into their attack positions. The sentries on the hill had no idea that an attack was coming until a sudden furious Athenian assault overwhelmed the defenders of the main fort. Most of the garrison discovered too late that their fort was under attack. Realizing that they could not now push the Athenians from the ramparts, most fled to the minor forts and quickly updated the garrisons there on recent events. The Athenian shock troops did not wait for the Syracusan response, but even as delegated troops set to work tearing down the western end of the cross-wall, other detachments were hurrying into position to meet the Syracusan stand-by force as it hurried out of the city.

The 600 Syracusans put up a brave fight, but they were against Athenian hoplites who, with the moon at their backs, appeared as a huge shadowy army of unknown strength, more of which was appearing all the time. The Syracusans stood their ground for as long as was possible in the uncertain conditions, and then fled. This proved the best thing they could have done, because Demosthenes was determined that his attack should sweep over the entire hill, and he led his army in swift pursuit. The advantage of this tactic was demonstrated when Gylippus and whatever troops he had been able muster launched a half-hearted charge against the Athenian surge, and were scattered. But there was also a major disadvantage to this headlong rush by night. It was the first time that the Athenian reinforcements had been on Epipolae, and many units lost their cohesion as they hastened across the rough terrain in the dark.

In the confusion, it became harder to tell which side was which. Apart from the distinctive inverted V of the *Lambda* carried on Spartan shields, Greek shields usually identified the carrier rather than his city, and anyway shield motifs were hard to identify by moonlight. The result was that the Athenian attack broke into scattered bands chasing and sometimes being chased by Syracusans. Demosthenes had expected this, and as was usual in these circumstances had given his men a code word by which they could challenge and recognize each other in the confusion. However, such was the chaos on the hilltop that the challenge and response were uttered so often that the Syracusans quickly learned both.

Consequently, some of the smarter Syracusan units gave the watchword and escaped unharmed when challenged by a larger Athenian unit, and then demolished smaller groups of Athenians when those groups identified themselves by responding correctly. It helped that the Syracusans were native to the area and were more quickly able to identify their positions and, on occasion, their neighbours. The more cosmopolitan Athenian force was having trouble distinguishing its own components. The Corcyran and Argive elements in the attacking Athenian force were Dorians. As such, they sang battle hymns very similar to those that the expeditionary force was accustomed to hearing from the Syracusans, who were also Dorian. So what the Athenians took to be enemy battle hymns were on occasion sung by Dorian hoplites on their own side who were engaging the Syracusans. These hoplites were surprised and indignant when Ionian Athenians started attacking them from the flanks and rear, especially as in the dark it was hard to tell friend from foe, and the circumstances were hardly ideal for explaining the mix-up. On other occasions Dorians on the Athenian side were startled to find the Athenians alongside them fleeing in panic the moment they began their battle hymn, leaving them alone against the oncoming enemy.

What had started as an organized Athenian surge eastwards across Epipolae devolved into a huge disorganized mass of humanity still driving approximately in that direction. But for the soldiers in the front line, telling whether the person before them was friend or foe quite literally involved a wild stab in the dark. It took a contingent of Boeotian soldiery fighting on the Syracusan side to restore some order to the chaos. Correctly identifying the soldiers opposite them as Athenian they launched an organized and vigorous charge that routed their confused and somewhat demoralized opponents. This helped to rally the Syracusans in their vicinity and get them all moving in the same direction, while the Athenians had the problem of working out if the figures running at them in the moonlight were attacking foes or retreating friends.

It did not help that though the Boeotians had reversed the tide of battle in their immediate locality, the Athenians were still advancing elsewhere. Consequently, at that point in the struggle any given unit might be moving east or west, or if confused by the terrain, north or south. As the Syracusans moved forward they began to form something resembling an organized battle line, and this turned the tide of the struggle. Now the flow moved west, with the Syracusan ranks becoming more coherent even as the Athenians continued to lose cohesion. Demosthenes was trying to keep together a new army fighting in unfamiliar conditions on a hill he had never been on before. Gylippus was fighting with troops he knew (and who knew each other) on terrain he and his men knew well. Once the advantage of surprise was spent, the circumstances had always favoured the Syracusans, and now this began to tell.

It was plain that the attack on the cross-wall had failed. Yet getting the Athenian army off Epipolae was no easy proposition. For a start it appears that Demosthenes had used the tactic of bypassing enemy strongpoints rather than overwhelming them, on the assumption that if his attack succeeded, these could be mopped up later.[54] Now the minor forts complicated the task of getting the army off the heights. Successfully disengaging an army from combat was one of the most difficult manoeuvres an ancient general could undertake. The magnitude of the task Demosthenes faced in disengaging his army was compounded by the fact that while the army as a whole was in general retreat, some units were still going forward (or sideways), and these risked being destroyed piecemeal. Even those units that withdrew successfully had problems. The passage off the hill was narrow and easily choked by too many men cramming into it at once, yet the hostile garrisons of the Syracusan forts and the advancing Syracusan army made the Athenians disinclined to form an orderly queue.

Many of the Athenians were new arrivals, and being unfamiliar with the terrain, they decided to make their own way down the sides of Epipolae. Veterans of the first expedition who took this option knew the few safe paths down the hill, and just as importantly, how to get to the Athenian camp once they reached level ground. The Athenian reinforcements were not so fortunate. Many took the wrong route and ended up trapped on the hill while many unfortunates fell to their deaths. Those who did reach the plain were disorientated from a night charging around the mountain and had no idea where they were.

It says much for Demosthenes' skill as a general that he managed to extricate at least part of his force from the hill in good order, and it says much for the discipline and morale of the Athenian hoplites that many of those who were not part of the organized retreat still found their way back to the Athenian camp over the next twelve hours. It also helped that the same narrow passage that had impeded the Athenian withdrawal from the hill also constricted the Syracusan advance, especially as Demosthenes would have arranged a rearguard to further slow the enemy descent.

Deliberations after a defeat

The morning dawned on a tired and dispirited Athenian army. Where once the expedition had almost effortlessly won victory after victory, now nothing seemed to be going right. The Syracusans gleefully helped themselves to the armour and other spoils of victory on Epipolae, while their cavalry roamed the countryside, cutting down those unfortunate Athenians who had been unable to find their way to their camp before daylight. Overall, the unsuccessful attempt on the cross-wall had cost some 2,000 lives. Apart from the wounded, there were many others who had made it to safety at the cost of abandoning all their gear, and as these men lacked armour or weapons they too had to be placed among the ineffectives.

As well as the wounded and the weaponless, there was an ever-increasing number of sick. No ancient army did well in this regard if it remained encamped in one place for long. Insanitary latrine arrangements spread disease, and even in the rare cases where proper latrine trenches were dug, the daily digestive output of several thousand men eventually worked its way into the groundwater. It did not help that the Athenian camp was next to a marsh, and anyway, the proximity of Syracusan cavalry at the Olympieum made travelling for fresh water sometimes more lethal than drinking the stagnant material on hand.

Demosthenes stuck by his original contention: since the attack on the cross-wall had failed, it was time for the expedition to cut its losses and go. Yet at the meeting called to arrange the best way to arrange a withdrawal he met with determined opposition. One might have expected Eurymedon to oppose the withdrawal. He had after all been among the commanders of the Athenian force operating in Sicily back in 426, which had been booted off the island when Hermocrates rallied the Greek cities against them. Eurymedon had been heavily fined by the Athenian assembly for lack of effort on that occasion, and could well imagine how much nastier the reaction at home would be this time around.

However, the main opponent to the idea of a withdrawal was Nicias. This was a complete about-face from the man who had never wanted the expedition to sail to Syracuse and who had never ceased to petition the assembly to bring him and his men home. Both Thucydides and Plutarch are clear that at least in part what explained Nicias's sudden reluctance to go home was that he shared Eurymedon's fear of what awaited him there. The Athenians had little patience with unsuccessful generals (as the exiled Thucydides well knew). For all the high hopes and huge expense that had accompanied the expedition at the outset, all that had been achieved was to firmly unite most of Sicily behind the Spartan cause.

Even if he pleaded ill-health it was probable that the best Nicias could hope for was a huge fine and exile. So in arguing against the withdrawal of the expedition, Nicias did exactly what had got the expedition into trouble in the first place – he dithered and delayed in the hope that circumstances would change for the better. He pointed out that the expedition had been sent with a mandate from the Athenian people. To pull out of Sicily would be directly contrary to that mandate and a dereliction of duty. Demosthenes was attempting to make a decision that was not his to make. If the expedition left Sicily, it must be because the Athenian people had re-called it.

Fine, replied Demosthenes. But the mandate from the Athenian people was to help Egesta and Leontini. There was nothing about conquering Syracuse in the original brief – that was something that previous leaders of the expedition had taken upon themselves. By all means let the expedition remain in Sicily. Catana still provided a friendly base, and there were several annoying minor cities on the island that the Athenians could crush for stress relief and profit. The fleet could get a decent re-fit and do some proper fighting outside the confines of that accursed harbour where the Syracusans had all the advantages. Why waste time, money and men by staying encamped pointlessly outside Syracuse?

Eurymedon was convinced, and voted with Demosthenes, but Nicias stubbornly refused to budge. The fact that he was so eager to remain outside a city that he had heretofore wanted only to see the back of made the other generals wonder. Did Nicias know something he was not telling them? Was he even now closing negotiations with traitors within Syracuse who were prepared to hand over the city to him? Perhaps even now a major Sicilian city was preparing to come over to the Athenian side. Finally and grudgingly, the generals agreed to delay their departure to see if Nicias had any rabbits to pull out of the hat.

They were encouraged in this decision by the fact that the Syracusans had made no attempt to follow up their victory on Epipolae. The Athenian force may have lost about a third of its reinforcements almost as soon as they arrived, but the remainder had still considerably increased the power of the forces at Nicias's disposal. For the moment the Syracusans were content to sit back behind their walls and allow disease to thin the Athenian ranks. This was particularly the case as Gylippus was away. Much as the Syracusans disliked the Spartan for his arrogance, his penny-pinching ways and his ill-concealed scorn for Syracusan manners and military ability, they knew full well that it was his steady hand that had plucked them out of the soup. While he was there 'they clustered around him like birds around an owl' (to use Plutarch's metaphor), and while he was gone they refrained from doing anything risky.

The fatal eclipse

Gylippus was not away for long. He had gone personally to take command of the substantial army that Syracusan recruiters had been collecting for him from cities across Sicily. Also he wanted to round up some hoplites sent in the spring from the Peloponnese. The merchantmen carrying these men had been blown off course and ended up in Libya. There the soldiers had borrowed two triremes from the city of Cyrene and after various minor adventures had finally arrived at Selinus, the city in the west of Sicily that the Athenians had originally come to the island to attack on behalf of Egesta.

Once he had gathered these reinforcements, Gylippus led them into Syracuse. The sight of these men arriving was an argument more powerful than anything Demosthenes had been able to muster. The Syracusans were now stronger than ever, while many in the Athenian army were incapacitated by illness. The ships of the fleet had been battered in a series of naval battles and badly needed overhaul and repair. The rowers were in equally bad shape. Mercenary rowers had continued to substitute locally seized slaves for themselves, and the trierarchs had to accept this, as the alternative was to have the men simply desert without leaving anyone in their place. It took 170 men to row a trireme, and the rowers were a mixture of Athenians, subject allies and mercenaries. It was customary for rowers to be paid only half their salary during a campaign and for them to collect the rest once the ship had returned to Athens and was decommissioned.

This measure was designed to prevent desertion, but it was only effective if there was a realistic chance of the ship getting back to Athens. Athenian rowers probably stuck with their ships through thick and thin. Allies faced exile from their cities if they abandoned their duty, but many probably thought this was the lesser of two evils. With the situation deteriorating by the day, many mercenary rowers appear to have simply written off their lost salary and departed to seek safer, more comfortable and less hazardous employment. And the Spartans were hiring, being quietly flush with cash, which the Persians were secretly subsidizing them.

Even Nicias had to accept that the splendid force which had sailed from the Piraeus over two years ago was long past its best. Nicias may not have wanted to go, but he was now a minority of one. Putting matters to a vote would simply have shown how isolated he was in his stance, so Nicias simply gave the orders that the men should start packing to depart. It is fairly clear that these orders were given some time around 25 August 413 BC. It would have taken at least two days to get everything ready, but giving the orders too far in advance of the planned departure would make it certain that the Syracusans got wind of the departure plans. The last thing Nicias wanted was for his loaded transports to have to fight their way off the island. As had happened before, a series of coincidences now neatly confounded the best laid-plans of the Athenians.

The departure date had been set for 28 August. We know this because Thucydides tells us, 'When everything was ready and the fleet was on the point of departing, there was an eclipse of the moon.' Since eclipses are datable astronomical events, and it is clear from the text of Thucydides that this was in the late summer of 413, the eclipse of August 27 must be the date in question.

At this time the restless minds of the Athenians had been grappling with the question of eclipses. The days when an eclipse was simply considered a sign from the gods were on the wane. The mental environment of the Athenians was moving from a universe where everything was directly managed by the gods to something closer to the modern idea of the universe as a machine where most natural phenomena are explicable by the interaction of the parts of the 'machine', so the Athenians had pretty much worked out that solar eclipses were caused by the moon coming between the sun and the earth. Plutarch tells the story of how Pericles was on the verge of sailing to war when a solar eclipse took place. When his timorous helmsman refused to sail in such literally ominous circumstances, Pericles held his cloak bundled up before the man's face and patiently explained that what was blocking the sunlight was something like his cloak, but much larger and further away.[55]

The problem with understanding solar eclipses was that it made lunar eclipses all the more inexplicable and therefore terrifying. If the earth was the centre of the solar system (as the Greeks believed) and a solar eclipse was caused by the moon getting between the earth and the sun, then what caused a lunar eclipse?

The idea that the shadow on the moon might be that of the earth itself had occurred to philosophers in Ionia, and in the 430s an Athenian astronomer called Meton had worked out that the lunar calendar was linked to the solar calendar in a nineteen-year cycle, a concept that once fully understood would make lunar eclipses as predictable as the solar variety. So in 413 the Athenians had all the data needed to make sense of a lunar eclipse, but their intellectual revolution was still so young that they had not yet joined up all the dots. For contemporary Greeks, the causes and timing of lunar eclipses were still worryingly vague, and the fact that one had occurred just as the fleet was about to take the momentous step of leaving Syracuse smacked of divine intervention.

Thucydides knew and respected Nicias and is perhaps kinder to him than his record warrants, but even Thucydides has to admit that his man was 'over-fond of divination'. On beholding the eclipse, Nicias immediately consulted with his soothsayers and announced that not only were the Athenians staying, but there would not even be any discussion of what was to happen next 'until thrice nine days had passed', that is, three times the sacred number three multiplied by three, which came rather neatly to a lunar month.[56]

This was folly, and greater folly than even the usual dictates of superstition demanded, for by tradition inexplicable heavenly phenomena made their meaning clear within three days. That Nicias decided to wait so much longer some historians explain by the death of Stillbedes, the professional soothsayer who had accompanied Nicias to Syracuse. By this account, while he was alive, Stillbedes had managed to restrain Nicias's irrational superstition, but now he was dead, Nicias had decided to make triply sure he was doing the right thing.

Just as likely is the probability that Nicias still did not want to go back to face the music in Athens and he seized on the eclipse as divine justification for a plan of action he wanted to follow anyway. There were perfectly rational reasons for holding out for another month, which had nothing to do with the moon. The most practical of these was money. Athens still had plenty and Syracuse did not. The strain of fighting the Athenians for two years was taking its toll on the Syracusan treasury – the city was 2,000 talents in debt (to put this in perspective, it took an average skilled artisan nine years of work to earn a talent of silver).

The city magistrates had tapped out both their municipal and personal lines of credit and now relied on donations from their allies. They, like the Athenians, had to pay for a large fleet, and for mercenaries both to row part of their fleet and to add numbers to their army. They also had fortifications such as the Olympieum and the forts on Epipolae to man and maintain in a hostile environment. If money made up the sinews of war, it was clear that the Syracusan war machine was on the verge of being hamstrung.

Furthermore, there were those in Syracuse who feared that their city's close ties with Sparta put their democratic constitution at risk, especially as the stock of Hermocrates and the oligarchic faction was riding high after recent victories. After all, it took only a few disgruntled citizens to betray a postern gate or a tower, and in consequence cities had, and would continue to be, taken in this manner throughout antiquity.

If the Athenians managed to hold on a bit longer, and if they finally broke the current string of defeats with a victory or two, Syracusan morale might buckle. Even if this led to a negotiated peace, Nicias would have something to take home that would save his neck, especially as another month would take the war close to the end of the campaigning season, when some kind of withdrawal from the present – and highly unhealthy camp – could be explained as a logical response to the prevailing strategic situation. And if nothing else, the Athenians had been sitting under the walls of Syracuse for the past two summers. What could go wrong in another twenty-seven days?

Fate had prepared the answers to that. Over the coming weeks, Nicias would find the detailed answer unfolding remorselessly, with each detail written in Athenian blood and suffering. The short answer was that things could go horribly, catastrophically wrong. In fact, the chance happenings of the death of a soothsayer and an unexpected eclipse would directly lead to the destruction of the expedition and the ruin of Athens. Perhaps the soothsayers consulted by Nicias should have taken Nemesis into account.

The decisive battle
The wheel had come full circle. The Syracusans, once cowed by defeat and desperately looking for a way to save their city, were brimming with confidence after a string of victories and intent on total victory. It was the

demoralized Athenians who were desperately trying to save themselves and their army. Nor could Athenian hoplites any longer take it for granted that they were superior to their Syracusan counterparts. Two years of training and practical experience had done wonders for Syracusan martial ability and morale, and victories such as that recently won on Epipolae had helped greatly. In like manner Syracusan triremes, which had once lurked in their shipyards afraid to be caught at sea by the dreaded Athenian navy, now aggressively prowled the harbour positively looking for a fight – and giving their crews extra training while they were about it.

It was symptomatic of the current situation that when the Syracusans advanced on the Athenian fortifications soon after the eclipse they easily crushed and killed the soldiers in the mixed force of infantry and cavalry that came out to meet them.

In the waters of the harbour the day after this minor action, seventy-six ships sailed against the Athenian fleet. Once the Syracusans would have considered odds of two-to-one in their favour a dangerous proposition, so much did they fear Athenian seamanship. Yet now, even though eighty-six Athenian triremes faced them, it was the Syracusans who rowed confidently into action. This was despite the fact that the Athenian ships included fresh triremes from Athens, which were fully seaworthy. It was probably these latter ships that Eurymedon took on a bold dash around the left flank of the advancing Syracusans in the hope of attacking from two sides at once.

This would have left the more decrepit veteran ships of the earlier Athenian expedition in the centre, and the Syracusans made short work of these. The speed with which the centre was crushed left Eurymedon trapped in the narrow space between the Syracusan fleet and a hostile shore – yet another example of how the close confines of the harbour restricted the usually flamboyant Athenian talent for manoeuvre. Eurymedon never stood a chance. His ships were smashed against the shore, and he himself was killed.

Gylippus saw the Athenian rowers abandoning their damaged vessels on the beach and hurried his land troops to deal with them. At this point the Etruscan troops who had joined the Athenians finally made their mark on the battlefield. The Syracusans had been running up in no sort of order and were easily scattered by the Etruscans in battle formation. What had started as a naval action shifted to the beach. Even in battle order, a trireme had positive buoyancy. When rammed and abandoned the ship might get swamped and made unseaworthy, but it would not actually sink. This is why, to the frustration of naval archaeologists, no wreck of a trireme has ever been found. Therefore the ships knocked out of action were still drifting near the beach, and because of that same positive buoyancy, sometimes in only a few feet of water. Gylippus wanted the wrecks before the Athenians could retrieve them and patch them up, so he fed increasing numbers of troops into the fray. The Athenians knew that without their warships they had little chance of leaving Syracuse, and fought passionately to keep them. So fiercely did they fight for the ships that eventually the Syracusans backed off and tried to destroy the wrecks by floating a fireship down on them. The Athenians were sailors with years of experience at this sort of thing, and the burning merchantman was easily fended off. Most of the wrecks were hauled back to the Athenian camp and total disaster was averted. But even a mitigated disaster was nevertheless a disaster. Eighteen ships had been lost and their crews killed, and what once would have seemed incredible was established as a simple, stark fact – the Syracusan fleet was better than the Athenian.

At about this time news of the planned Athenian withdrawal reached the citizens of Syracuse. Far from being delighted, the Syracusans determined to do everything in their power to stop their unwelcome guests from leaving. Firstly, they had no wish to see the Athenians withdraw to a friendly base such as Catana and return the following summer refreshed and invigorated. But secondly, and more importantly, the Syracusans reckoned that they had the beating of the Athenians well in hand, and wanted their enemy to stick around so that they could finish the job.

It had been decades since anyone had handed the Athenians a major defeat. The genius and daring of the Athenian people had chased the Persians back to Asia Minor and frustrated the military prowess of Sparta. It occurred to the Syracusans that they were set to succeed where these two mighty powers had failed. Nothing appealed to an ancient Greek character so much as a chance for glory, and demolishing the vaunted Athenian expedition would be glorious indeed.

> If they could beat the combined forces of the Athenians, both on land and sea, it would be an achievement that would make them famous throughout the Hellenic world … Great would be their honour, not only among those of the present generation, but with future generations also.
>
> Thuc. 7.56

With this thought in mind, the Syracusans set about closing off the mouth of the Great Harbour so as to make it impossible for the Athenians to sail away. This was no easy task, for as described earlier (p.99), the mouth of the harbour was over three-quarters of a mile wide. No mere chain could be stretched across such a gap (this being the usual way of closing off a harbour in antiquity), so the Syracusans decided to use a chain of ships instead. Both merchant vessels and triremes badly battered by recent events were moored across the harbour mouth and connected by chains. The completed barrier demonstrated the sort of imaginative improvisation at which the Athenians excelled, and it must have been with some chagrin that they now experienced it used against themselves.

The chagrin was all the more acute because their commanders had done the equivalent of cancelling the milk delivery in the expectation of moving out. They had told supply ships to stop coming in from Catana, and now that the harbour mouth was blocked, deliveries could not be resumed. The Athenians were on the verge of running out of provisions.

Nicias, when his back was against the wall and he had no option but to act, was actually quite a good general. He simply lacked the self-confidence that would have made him a great one and was so afraid of failure that he preferred to do nothing at all. But no one had to explain to him what the barrier across the mouth of the harbour meant. He was indeed out of options. Quite simply, the Athenians had to break the barrier or they were finished. The only escape was by sea, and if the Athenian expedition could not reach the sea, there was no escape at all. So, after having prevaricated his army to the brink of disaster, Nicias acted decisively and promptly. He pulled the army away from the fortifications and established a camp just large enough to hold the army's stores and sick. Even these were readied for immediate embarkation if the chance presented itself.

Then Nicias gathered everything in the Athenian force that floated and prepared to load it with soldiers and point it at the harbour mouth. Eurymedon had tried and died while attempting subtlety by sea. Nicias would not be as delicate. The point of the coming battle would not be to defeat the Syracusan navy; it would be to break the harbour barrier. Since a desperate Syracusan defence of that barrier could be expected, the best way to take the blockading ships would be for the Athenians to load their own ships with every soldier they could carry and try to sweep over the enemy by force of numbers. Given the amount of archers, javelineers and infantry involved, the coming struggle would be something close to a land battle with ships underfoot.

Both sides were perfectly clear about the stakes. Nicias addressed his men before the fight, and made the point unambiguously. 'You are fighting for your lives,' he told them. Succeed and you will soon be home once more. Fail, he said, 'And you will be at the mercy of the Syracusans, and they know how we intended to treat them when we first attacked.' Nor were the men fighting only for themselves. Athens had put everything into her final surge of reinforcements. At home 'there are no more ships in the dockyards, no more soldiers in reserve'.[57] Even if the expedition had failed to take Syracuse, the ships and men were going to be needed to stop Sparta from taking Athens. The Athenian army had to get home to save the city – it was no exaggeration to say as went the coming battle, so would go the war.

Gylippus pointed out to his men that they were in a happy position. If they won, the enemy and the threat to their city would be crushed. If the Syracusans lost, their enemy planned to run away. It was difficult to think of a really negative outcome. Therefore, the army should go into battle joyously, yet with fury in their hearts. Here was an enemy who had attacked without provocation and with the intention of enslaving them. It was time to prove the proverb that the greatest of all pleasures lay in extracting just vengeance.

> For all of you know that these are not mere enemies, but mortal foes. Men who came here to enslave, to inflict bitter grief upon the men and outrage on your women and children ... We fight for something worth fighting for; to punish the aggressor and restore Sicily to liberty.
>
> Gylippus in Thuc. 7.68

The Spartan general had noted the Athenian intention to fight the coming battle almost as an infantry action, and had enough confidence in the seamanship of those in his command to partly decline that option. If the Athenians were going into battle fully loaded with soldiers, he would out-sail them. A trireme was top-heavy in the water at the best of times. With the decks loaded with infantrymen, the Athenian ships were positively unstable. It was also apparent that the Athenian focus was the barrier across the harbour. Therefore the ships that made up the barrier were stacked with soldiers grimly aware that it was they who were to bear the brunt of the desperate Athenian attack.

The non-blockading warships were not set to meet the Athenians head-on. Instead they were to fight the sort of conventional naval action for which the heavily laden Athenian ships were ill-prepared. Gylippus was trusting that his blockade ships would be able to take the first impact of the Athenian assault. Thereafter those warships that had avoided the first charge were to close in on the Athenian fleet as it packed itself tightly against the blockade and hit it hard on the flanks and rear. That way, if the Athenians did break the blockade line, the Syracusans would forcibly usher them out of the harbour and into the open sea. But if the line held, as the Syracusans devoutly hoped it would, the Athenians would be caught like rats in a trap. Just to make absolutely sure of this, Gylippus stationed the Syracusan army along the shoreline so that any Athenian ships that recoiled from the blockade could not beach and allow the crews to make their own way back to the Athenian camp.

In his turn, Nicias did the same, lining every man not on the warships along the limited shoreline that the Athenians still held. This provided a haven for any ships that made it back to the Athenian lines but also acknowledged that all Greeks fought better with an audience. Any deeds of heroism or cowardice would be seen and acknowledged by the entire army. For the same reason, it is certain that every Syracusan who could crowded the ramparts on the city walls to watch the battle. Whatever the outcome, history would be made this day.

So it was that on a fateful late summer morning Demosthenes led out the 110 ships that contained most of the Athenians' army and all of their hopes. They rowed grimly straight for the barrier, where Pythen and his contingent of Corinthian ships waited to meet them. To left and right of the Athenian thrust were separate wings of the Syracusan fleet, the one commanded by an admiral called Sicanus and the other under one Agatharchus. Overall the Syracusan side had fewer effective ships – some seventy-six of them – but these effectives were fresher, better adapted for the conditions and more, well, effective.

Not unexpectedly, while the opening phase of the battle went according to the Syracusan plan, thereafter the battle took on a momentum of its own. Though they came close to breaking, and were actually overwhelmed at points, the Syracusans on blockade line overall withstood the first furious Athenian assault. The Syracusan fleet duly charged the flanks as planned, but it appears that the Athenians were too skilled at naval warfare not to have anticipated this to some extent. Certainly the blows from left and right were much less effective than Gylippus had hoped. Perhaps the Athenians had some lightly-manned ships securing the flanks, or perhaps some warships had been armoured for just this eventuality. In either case, the plans of both generals now broke down, and the battle devolved into a chaotic struggle between the troops on the water.

For the Athenian steersmen, accustomed to guiding their ships into action across the open sea, the battle in the harbour was a nightmare. There was seldom space to ram an opponent, and even when an enemy was successfully rammed there was often no space behind to back water and disengage afterwards. The sheer density of the fight was such that instead of either attacking or preparing to repel boarders, a helmsman might find his efforts divided between pressing home an attack against the ship to port while simultaneously trying to fend off an assault on the starboard side – and do this all the while under a constant rain of arrows, javelins and slingshot.

For Thucydides, and therefore according to those whom he undoubtedly interviewed, one aspect of the battle seared into the memory of the participants was the sheer noise. No ancient battle was a quiet affair, as swords crash against shields, commanders bellow orders, and individual soldiers cry out in pain, encouragement or pure battle-lust. But added to this was the din of ships colliding and the cries of helmsmen and trierarchs as they battled the chaos and tried to inspire their men. Then, far louder than the waves slapping the ships' keels, came the roar of the thousands upon thousands lining the city walls and shore. The spectators were helpless to intervene in the battle that was to shape their destiny, but each urged their side on, cheering each success and groaning at each setback.

> Impressions were different, depending from where one watched from the shore. From the perspective of some, their side was winning. They were encouraged by the sight, and called on the gods not to snatch salvation from them. Others saw where their side was being defeated, and they cried out in grief, being more downcast by the sight than were the men doing the actual fighting ... So sounds of all kinds could be heard from the watching Athenian army – yells of despair and of triumph, shouts of 'we are winning' and counter-cries of 'we are losing'; and all the variety of exclamations to be expected of a huge army in great peril.
>
> Thuc. 7.71

The battle raged for a long time. The Athenians were desperate and the Syracusans were stubborn, and neither was prepared to give an inch. But gradually it became apparent that the cries from the watchers on the shore were more triumphant on the Syracusan side, and more despairing and grief-stricken from the Athenians. The attack on the blockade had long ago lost its momentum. Now, in one individual fight after another, the Syracusans were beginning to prevail, with every minor victory making available more resources to bring to the next struggle, until finally the remaining Athenians were overwhelmed.

The surviving Athenian ships broke from the battle line and rowed hard for the shelter of the Athenian-held shore accompanied by the triumphant yells of the Syracusans and the lamentations of the Athenians on the beach. A good number of Athenian ships floated rudderless in the water, rammed or swamped and those aboard dead or prisoner. The others were intent only on reaching the safest possible shore. As soon as they beached, the ships were abandoned by soldiers and crew who scattered in flight for the safety of the Athenian lines. The ships themselves represented the last solid chance that the Athenians would get safely back to their homes, but now they lay derelict on the beach for the victorious enemy to collect at their leisure.

Those crewmen who made it back to the Athenian camp were well aware that their refuge was only temporary. They were sheltering in a weakened, disease-ridden camp without food, without supplies, and without any realistic chance of escape. Some of the stronger-minded veterans made their way back to the walls of the camp and began to prepare a hopeless defence against the attack that would surely come once the Syracusans had rallied from their victory.

Others, stunned by grief and despair, remained on the shore, fully aware of the uselessness of anything they could now attempt. Some individuals began making plans to desert or otherwise save themselves, and saw little shame in that. Whatever became of the men in its ranks, the Athenian expedition had finished in utter, abject failure.

Chapter 10

The End

Pity, yes, let there be pity now for those about to die, who once led the Greeks in war

Euripides l. 1183 Orestes c.408

Athenian morale had been completely broken by the failed attack on the blockade. Only the indomitable Demosthenes kept his nerve. He pointed out to his devastated colleagues that the Syracusans had seen intensely hard fighting and were exhausted. Instead of following up his success, Gylippus had merely allowed his army to collect its dead, take the wrecked triremes in tow and head back to the city. A quick prow-count of the beached triremes told the Athenian general that Athens could still muster sixty ships, while after the casualties they had taken in the close-run fight the Syracusans only had about fifty.

That very moment, said Demosthenes, was the time for the Athenians to re-board their ships and go right back at the blockade. The Syracusans would not be expecting it. They might not be prepared to go through a second round and could simply let the Athenians go by. And if they didn't, well, exactly what did the expedition have to lose?

His exhortations were to no avail. The Athenians, so vaunting, ambitious and persevering in success, simply had too little experience at coping with failure. Almost everything had come right in the end for their army and their city for as long as they could remember. Consequently, the Athenians had battled gamely against the constant setbacks and defeats of recent months, certain that, as always, they would eventually emerge triumphant. Now it was very clear that this time there would be no such result and this realization utterly demoralized the army. Not only could Demosthenes not prevail upon his men to re-board the ships, but the broken men of the expedition could not even gather the energy to go out and collect their dead in the customary truce that followed a battle.

Just to make things even more galling for Demosthenes, later events showed that he was probably right. Hermocrates was about the only Syracusan who wanted to follow up hard on the success in the harbour. He reckoned that once the Athenians had been repelled from the Syracusan blockade, their only chance would be a rapid breakout by land. He urged his fellow commanders to get the army moving out of the city and blocking the roads that the Athenians would take. These included both the northern road to Gela and the route past Epipolae into the interior. If the Athenian army made a dash up either road during the night, the Syracusans might yet find the enemy entrenched in the interior and still a threat.

But Hermocrates enjoyed as little success at getting the Syracusans moving as Demosthenes had done with the Athenians. The Syracusans had fought heroically and were drunk with success. That day was a festival of that favourite Dorian hero, Heracles, and to celebrate it the Syracusans wanted to get drunk the conventional way as well. In short, though for very different motives, the protagonists on either side were not inclined to move, successful though a move would probably be. Hermocrates did the best he could. He gathered some sympathetic cavalry colleagues and sent them to within earshot of the Athenian camp.

The cavalrymen pretended to be well-wishers of the Athenians and told them not to move. The horsemen claimed that what Hermocrates had wanted had in fact become reality, informing the despairing Athenians that the Syracusan army had in fact surged out of the city and were even now barricading roads out of the area. The recent and painful night action on Epipolae might have been mentioned as a further incentive for the Athenians to stay put. It would be best, the 'well-wishers' urged, for the Athenians to rest overnight and attempt their breakout in the morning, when they were fresher and could see what was going on.

The Athenian sentries duly carried these messages to their commanders. It would be no surprise if Nicias followed the advice to the letter. Inactivity was his preferred state, and he knew that the Athenians genuinely did have supporters within Syracuse, so intelligence such as that conveyed by the sentries was unsurprising, even if unwelcome. On the other hand, it is quite possible that the Athenians would not have fled that night even if genuine messages had arrived telling that the roads were wide open. The army was utterly dispirited and too apathetic to move. The Athenians did not stir the next day either. Their camp remained sunk in torpor even as the Syracusans got industriously to work. Barricades now sprang up unopposed across the major roads and ambushes were prepared at leisure on minor roads and river crossings. The sailors of the Syracusan fleet busied themselves burning and towing away the remainder of the Athenian fleet, and neither sword nor javelin was raised to stop them.

It was two days before Athenian spirits recovered to the point where the army was prepared to attempt an escape. However he felt personally, Nicias did a general's part in trying to keep his men motivated in the face of near-certain defeat. He pointed out that the Athenians were still a formidable force of some 40,000 men. Any army of that size had to consider that it had a fighting chance.

Nicias – or Thucydides – exaggerates here. The figure of 40,000 can just about be reached by adding every hoplite, light infantryman, sailor and servant who had crossed to Sicily. However, for Nicias to be believed, one must make the gratuitously false assumption that the fierce fighting and illnesses to date had produced no casualties worth reckoning.

Nicias, though, was well aware that many in his army were suffering from wounds, illness and hunger. He pointed out that he himself had been sick and had suffered the same ills as the rest of the expedition, yet he was still prepared to soldier on. He had a point. Just a generation later, a force less than half the size of the expedition would find itself in equally hostile circumstances on the other side of the ancient world. These 10,000 Greek mercenaries went to Asia Minor to support the bid of the pretender Cyrus for the Persian throne. Leaderless after defeat in battle, the 10,000 nevertheless kept their cohesion and marched hundreds of miles through hostile terrain to the sea.[58] It could be done, if the army had the will to do it.

Politically, too, the Athenians stood a fighting chance. There were many who had reservations about what would happen if Syracuse became the undisputed hegemon of the island. Some Sicilian city-states had been lukewarm or hostile to Syracusan pleas for help when it looked as though the city would fall to the Athenians. These now needed an insurance policy in case the Syracusans decided to pay off their grudges, and keeping the Athenian army in play would provide exactly that assurance. This was even more true of the native Sicels of the interior, who had to a large extent thrown their lot in with the Athenians. These were eager to have Athenian protection against Syracusan revenge.

The interior of Sicily was therefore the immediate destination of the soldiers of the defeated expedition. Nicias and Demosthenes fussed around the army as it fell into formation, making sure that the hoplites dressed properly in their ranks and presented a military appearance, no matter what their inward feelings. The soldiers of the expedition would march in a hollow square, with non-combatants in the middle along with such useful baggage as could be salvaged. Ancient accounts of the retreat give no clear indication of the original destination of the army. From Thucydides it is clear that the intention was to cut into the interior and gain immediate relief and reinforcement from the Sicels, who had been requested to have immediate stocks of food laid on for the expedition's arrival. From there, perhaps the army would loop northwards with the intention of finding haven at Catana. When in a secure base once more, the generals could work out their next step at leisure.

This was not a bad plan, but did not take into account that the Syracusans would not simply sit and watch their unwelcome visitors depart. Rather, Hermocrates and Gylippus intended to do everything in their power to destroy the expedition while they had the chance, and the men under their command were desperately eager to get started on that project.

The initial problem for the Syracusan generals was that they were uncertain of the direction the Athenian breakout would take. From necessity their forces were therefore thinly stretched to cover all the major and minor routes away from their city. When the Syracusans received word that the Athenians were marching towards the ford of the river Anapus, it was too late for Gylippus to concentrate his men, and he could do no more than hurry after his departing enemies. By the time Gylippus was on the move, the Athenians had brushed the guard on the ford aside, crossed the river and were striking for the interior.

Retreat from the Acrean Cliff

For the next two days the Athenians' march went well. Their first camp was on a defensible hill, and the next day they took a village,[59] which stood on level ground. After first stripping the village for much-needed supplies, the army camped there overnight. However, on the second day, the Athenians covered only 2 miles to the previous day's 4. Resistance was solidifying.

Almost from the start the Athenians were slowed and harassed by Syracusan cavalry while Gylippus struggled to get his army out in front of the retreating Athenian expedition. Necessary though it was, the delay required for the Athenians to strip the village gave Gylippus the chance he needed. By now it was clear that the Athenians were heading for the interior, and an obvious choke point lay not far from the village. This was a gully up between two hills with sides so steep that the place was known to locals as the Acrean Cliff. The Athenians would have to traverse this gully if they were to continue on their way, and what would already be a hard climb was made more difficult by cavalry who harassed the army's flanks as the men approached the obstacle and javelineers who bombarded the Athenians as they ascended. Discouraged, the Athenians gave up and fell back on the village they had occupied the previous day.

Early the next morning the Athenians tried again. They had little choice. They were now desperately short of supplies and had depleted the few provisions found in the village. However, the Syracusans had not rested on their laurels overnight. They had been building, reinforcing and bringing up heavy infantry. Where the previous day the difficulty had been massed ranks of javelineers, the attacking Athenians now had to surmount a low wall backed by locked ranks of hoplites. A crossing that would once have been immensely difficult yesterday was now totally impossible. It is a measure of Athenian despair that the army kept trying despite this. The failure of that day's attempt was made all the more inevitable by an autumnal storm, which slowed the Athenian attack and further damaged morale.

Though the storm had presumably eased the problem of supplying the army with water, food was now at a wretchedly low level, and this level sank further after yet another futile assault in which the army tried to find another way up the hill the following day. It was clear that the expedition could not go forward and could not stay where it was. The only solution was to go back and attempt another route. Gylippus had foreseen this, and he had soldiers building fortifications to prevent the Athenians from doing just that. Had the Athenians spent another day on their futile attempt to get through the gully, the defences to their rear would have strengthened to the point that the expedition would have been trapped. As it was, the Athenians were able to demolish the planned blockade in an afternoon action. Then that night the expedition's generals ordered the men to set up campfires as usual, but then pulled the army back under cover of darkness. The plan was to move back towards the sea and then, since the route to Catana was blocked, head into the interior by a different route with the intention of afterwards reaching the coast at either Camerina or Gela.

The night march took the Syracusans by surprise, and some of the more cynical types in the army accused Gylippus of deliberately allowing the Athenians to escape, presumably to extend his time in command. It did not take the vengeful Syracusans long to pick up the expedition's track. A large army leaves a conspicuous trail, and there would have been many country folk in the Syracusan ranks capable of following individual deer. The relief of the Athenians at escaping their persecutors lasted exactly a morning. By midday the Syracusans had caught up again. Or rather they had caught up with part of the Athenian army. The Athenian withdrawal had not gone completely to plan.

The section of the army led by Demosthenes consisted of 6,000 men. These had been charged with covering the retreat of the main force. They had organized a proper rearguard, which was prepared at any moment to convert their night retreat into a fighting withdrawal. Nicias meanwhile had led the rest of the army hell-for-leather out of the trap. His men were ordered to fight only when flight was impossible and concentrate on demolishing whatever obstacles the Syracusan army had raised to block their retreat. Consequently, with Demosthenes concentrating on battle-readiness and Nicias on swift movement, the two components of the army moved at very different speeds, with Demosthenes being appreciably slower. In the confusion of the night march, the two generals did not notice how far apart they were drawing from one another. By midday, when the Syracusans caught up with Demosthenes, Nicias and the rest of the army were some 6 miles away.

The last stand(s)

Poor communications meant that Demosthenes was unaware that most of the expedition was over the horizon and accelerating. Therefore when the Syracusans attacked his rearguard, he did the logical thing and formed into battle order. The terrain was suited to defence, being mainly olive trees surrounded by low walls, and the entire Athenian army would have had little problem holding off the Syracusans until the retreat could begin again. Indeed, the Syracusans had great respect for the military prowess of the Athenian hoplites. They had been bruised often enough in previous encounters to be wary of getting into close range. But then, they did not have to.

Without the contingent led by Nicias, the Athenian rearguard was small enough for the Syracusans to surround completely and prevent from escaping. Thereafter, the Syracusans tried to wear the Athenians down by staying out of spear-reach and resuming the javelin bombardment of previous days. This went less well than planned. The Athenians had their backs to the wall – given the nature of the terrain, they sometimes literally had their backs to a wall – and were prepared to die fighting.

Seeing that the army was making little headway, Gylippus and his generals chose to offer an escape – for some. Heralds approached the exhausted Athenian rearguard and offered freedom to those allies whom the Athenians had conscripted into their expedition. Some of these 'allies' had not wanted to be on the expedition in the first place and were not unexpectedly disillusioned by the way matters had developed. Once contingents from some of the subject cities of the Athenian empire came forward and surrendered, the rest of Demosthenes' men realized that their situation was hopeless, and sought the best terms they could get. These were basically that they would not be killed nor starved to death. Otherwise, the 6,000 under Demosthenes surrendered unconditionally to the mercy of the people they had once sought to enslave. This surrender was apparently a grass-roots initiative. According to Plutarch, Demosthenes was prepared to fight to the death and only abandoned the struggle when he saw the Syracusans closing in on him. Even then he tried to run himself through with his own sword. But he had left it too late, and the Syracusans managed to take their prize prisoner alive.

Meanwhile, Nicias had fought his way clear of the surrounding Syracusan forces and encamped his army on a hill overlooking the river Erinus. He may have been pleased at the ease with which he had managed his escape. If so, his pleasure was soured by the news – brought by gleeful Syracusan heralds – that the reason he had fought clear so easily was because the main Syracusan force had been preoccupied with surrounding and capturing Demosthenes and his men. Nicias refused to believe the truth of these reports until the Syracusans allowed him to send a horseman to report back personally.

The Syracusans were in no hurry. They needed to bring up the rest of their army and knew that the Athenians on their hilltop were suffering intensely from thirst. In the same spirit of delay, they embarked on leisurely negotiations, all the while making sure that the Athenians remained waterless. They offered Nicias and his men the same terms as those on which Demosthenes had surrendered. Nicias countered with an offer that, if the Athenians were allowed to go free, Athens would reimburse the Syracusans their costs for the war and give hostages until the money was raised. This offer was rejected with contempt, quite possibly because the Syracusans knew that after funding the expedition and the substantial reinforcements sent in that losing cause, Athens did not have that kind of money available. In any case, the siege and repeated battles in recent years had left many Syracusans dead, and their grieving families wanted the Athenian invaders to pay in ways that did not involve cash.

That night, Nicias tried another silent retreat, but this time the Syracusans were ready and waiting. Some 300 men did break through the Syracusan lines (they were captured later), but the rest of the army remained on the hillside, tormented by thirst.

The following day Nicias led his men towards the river at the bottom of the valley. So desperate were his men for water that they did not so much want to cross the river as to drink it. Again, we have Thucydides to thank for what is probably an eyewitness account of the terrible scenes that followed.

They rushed down to the river, and threw discipline to the winds when they got there ... The opposite bank was steep. From there a host of Syracusan javelineers rained missiles down on the Athenians. These were a confused herd, intent only on greedily drinking from the deep river. Even when the Peloponnesians came down to them and started slaughtering them – especially those actually in the river – they went on drinking. The water became muddied and polluted with blood, nevertheless the Athenians fought only against each other as they struggled to get to it.

Thuc. 7.85ff.

The Athenian army simply disintegrated. There was no organized surrender such as the men of Demosthenes had negotiated. Many Athenians simply abandoned the army and made individual breaks for freedom. Those who escaped capture turned up in friendly cities – especially Catana – over the following weeks. Others were made prisoner and therefore impromptu slaves by the Syracusan soldiers who captured them. These were a relatively fortunate minority. Many more Athenians were simply cut down where they stood or as they attempted to flee. With the small river becoming clogged with the bodies of his men, Nicias surrendered himself to Gylippus, begging the Spartan general only to stop the slaughter.

The prisoners

Gylippus was happy enough to accept Nicias as a prisoner. He had hopes of taking both Demosthenes and Nicias back to Sparta with him. The Spartan people still had bitter memories of how Demosthenes had defeated and captured the best of their warriors on Pylos (p.16), and undoubtedly would be delighted to meet the Athenian general again in these different circumstances.

Yet just as the Spartans considered Demosthenes their most dangerous enemy, they considered Nicias a friend. This was the man who had negotiated a peace that had given them time to re-group after the first disastrous phase of the war and who had tried hard to keep that peace together. Nicias was certainly better off in Spartan hands than Syracusan.

There was something of a party atmosphere among the Syracusans on the river bank. Trees were used as trophy stands to display fine examples of Athenian armour and many cavalrymen concentrated on stripping the finery off the remnants of the Athenian cavalry and decorating themselves and their horses with the spoils.

It was some time before a disorganized column headed back to Syracuse, though with far fewer prisoners than had been expected. For a start, it had taken a long time for the order to take prisoners to register through the blood-lust that had gripped the Syracusan army. Then, once it was clear that taking prisoners was the order of the day, many soldiers were loath to hand in their new assets to the generals. Instead, captive Athenians were stashed wherever they could be hidden for eventual sale later. Unsurprisingly, many of these 'unofficial' prisoners managed then or afterwards to make a break for freedom, and these too eventually turned up at friendly Sicilian cities.

The thousand or so men formally captured suffered a grimmer fate. The city authorities were not sure what to do with them, and in the end the men were kept in the stone quarries, where many died of exposure and starvation from poor rations. The Syracusans allowed each prisoner a pint of barley meal and a half-pint of water a day (half the ration usually given to a slave). Their city was still suffering from the effects of a long siege and was almost bankrupt. No one was greatly interested in the welfare of the men who had brought them to this pass.

The one exception to the general neglect were those recent arrivals from Athens who knew some of the latest production of the playwright Euripides. Those who could quote the great poet's verses verbatim received in return lenient treatment from their culture-starved captors. But it was only some ten weeks later that the Syracusans organized themselves sufficiently to auction the other survivors off as slaves. The most hated of Syracuse's enemies – those from Athens itself and the Italiote Greeks who had joined their cause – were sold last, and suffered most in their miserable captivity. It is unlikely that the prisoners went for a high price. As Thucydides remarks, 'Sicily was full of them,' and the men from the quarry were now in the last extremities of suffering from their various misadventures.

There was a great debate about what to do with Nicias and Demosthenes, who were imprisoned together. Gylippus wanted to take both prisoners home with him, each for different reasons. The Syracusans wanted to keep them, though again their motives were mixed. Hermocrates argued that the only thing greater than victory was victory with moderation and that the generals should be spared. Others indignantly mentioned dead relatives and personal suffering and demanded that those who had instigated the attack on their island and city should pay with their lives. Gylippus had been respected because he was a canny battle-leader. Now that he was no longer needed, the Syracusans reviled the Spartan for the many defects in his character and totally disregarded his wishes. They made it clear that he would not be awarded custody of the captives.

There are mixed reports of what happened next. Plutarch quotes differing opinions of earlier historians, some of whom (including Thucydides) assert that the Syracusans put the pair to death. Others assert that Nicias and Demosthenes, anticipating their probable fate, managed to kill themselves first. The cynical Thucydides noted that Nicias had been in negotiations with prominent Syracusan sympathizers throughout the siege of their city. These sympathizers faced ruin – at best – if their treasonous dealings became public. Given that these prominent Syracusan citizens had the means, motive and opportunity to silence the most credible witnesses to their actions, the 'suicide' of Demosthenes and Nicias must indeed be considered with a certain skepticism.

No one hurried to tell the people of Athens. The reason for this rectitude was made clear when an unfortunate traveller turned up in the city assuming that its citizens had been updated with the news that was running like wildfire through the rest of the Greek world. Taking a seat in a barber-shop, he began to discuss developments in Sicily. He may have been surprised that his alarmed barber took off like a startled hare when the gist of the conversation became clear. The barber hurried to tell the city authorities, but stopped to pass on the alarming news in the Agora.

By then the traveller had wisely decided to fade into the background, leaving the barber with no one to verify his claims. He was charged with throwing the city into a panic and spreading malicious rumours. His punishment was severe torture, which was only remitted once official messengers arrived, bearing chapter and verse of the severity of the Athenian defeat and the veracity of the barber's claims.

Aftermath

Athens

The end of the Athenian expedition was not the end of the war. Though the men of the expedition were eventually broken by an unrelieved series of disasters, the people of Athens retained the indomitable spirit that had made their city great.

They threw their energies into building themselves a new fleet and unwisely demanded a substantial contribution from the subject peoples of their empire. The result was predictable. Even had there been considerable goodwill towards the Athenians before the start of the expedition (and this is dubious), the cost of sending men and reinforcements to Sicily had cost the

Athenian empire's subject people dear in money and blood. Athens had consciously chosen, with the selective destruction of communities such as Melos, to rule by terror. Now that the Athenians were less terrifying, the consequences were foreseeable. Many island states flatly refused to pay for a fleet which, if it succeeded in its intended purpose, would thereafter be used to subjugate them once more.

The mutiny was led by Euboea, Lesbos and especially Chios. It became evident that the Syracusans, urged on by Hermocrates, intended to send a fleet to the Aegean. The Spartans, now flush with Persian cash, also raised a fleet. Among the Spartan fleet's commanders was Alcibiades, who was very eager to get out of town since the king was becoming increasingly suspicious as to the parentage of his new son (p.82). The promise that they would not be left to the mercy of the Athenian fleet was enough to convince the waverers. Soon only the island of Samos remained within the empire that had once virtually spanned the Aegean and spread across the coast of Asia Minor. One of the most damaging defections was that of Rhodes. The island city state was among the last to desert Athens, but when it did join the forces arrayed against the city, it provided a reserve of sailors every bit as skilled as the Athenians themselves.

Athens fought on. The war became a series of naval actions fought out among the island states and the Anatolian coast. The strain of the long struggle began to wear down the Athenian democracy. With perfect hindsight, it was clear that the Sicilian expedition had been a huge mistake.

The men, money, ships and prestige that Athens now desperately needed had been squandered in a burst of *hubris* in a totally unnecessary gamble. The Athenians began to distrust the demagoguery that had 'tricked' the assembly into pouring so many of their resources down the Sicilian drain. Incredibly, the defector trickster-in-chief, Alcibiades, had the nerve to put himself at the forefront of this movement. He had decided that only a change of government would lead to his reinstatement in Athens. The Athenian people were desperate to believe that Alcibiades could bring the Persians over with him if he changed sides. Alcibiades assured them that this would not happen while the city was a democracy, as the Persian king distrusted this form of government.

So in the spring of 411 a revolution – part conspiracy, part popular movement – led to the overthrow of the world's leading democracy and its replacement with an oligarchy. This oligarchy failed in almost every item of its manifesto. The Persians did not come over to the Athenian side. Sparta was not persuaded to make peace with the Athenians, the steady stream of allied defections continued and the population on the home front became divided and resentful. Possibly the only substantial achievement of the coup was to alienate the once-loyal and thoroughly democratic Samoans. After just four months the oligarchs were overthrown and a moderate democracy reinstalled in its place. Alcibiades was again exiled, and could consider himself lucky to have escaped so lightly.

But all the while the Spartans were becoming more proficient at warfare by sea and the weight of Persian gold tipped the scales ever more in their direction. It occurred to the Spartans that the best way to choke Athenian resistance was to deny the city its grain supplies. Even before the loss of the farmlands of Attica, these had mainly been imported from friendly cities along the shores of the Black Sea. By blocking the Hellespont, the Spartans could interdict the grain convoys and finally make the siege of Athens effective. In part this was to force the Athenians to make peace.

Instead Sparta lost its fleet at Arginusae, and had lost another before that. Yet thanks to Persian funding, Sparta could afford to keep building more while Athens was straining its uttermost to keep its last ships at sea. When this last fleet was finally destroyed in a mismanaged naval action at Aegospotomai, it was the final devastating blow in a series of disasters that had started with the loss of the expedition to Sicily. Athens was besieged in earnest and was finally brought to surrender by a siege that saw much of the population die of hunger before the once-proud city admitted total defeat.

Sicily

Egesta and Selinus were still at loggerheads, and with their Athenian champions gone the Egestans turned for help to Carthage. They should have been careful what they wished for. Carthage had been biding its time, and with Athens gone, a huge Carthaginian army flattened Selinus, killed the inhabitants and marched on the rest of Sicily. Himera too was devastated, but thereafter the Sicilian Greeks realized that they faced a conqueror far crueller than the Athenians. They united and threw back the invaders. One casualty of the invasion was the Syracusan democracy. A soldier called Dionysus used the military emergency to seize power in the city and ruled as a tyrant thereafter.

That greatest of Syracusan patriots, Hermocrates, had also fallen out with the democrats and had been exiled in 412. He returned to his native city in 408 and took a not unexpectedly dim view of the rise of Dionysus. He was killed in a street fight in 407, the year before Dionysus seized supreme power.

Gylippus fared little better. Given charge of a consignment of silver for

Sparta, the formerly penny-pinching general upped his game and embezzled a goodly part of his precious cargo. He fled on discovery of his crime and was condemned to death *in absentia*.

Alcibiades eventually settled down in exile as a petty warlord in a fort in Thrace. No one was surprised when he was killed by unknown assassins in 404. Suspects included: the family of a local girl whom Alcibiades had allegedly violated; the Syracusans, Messenians and Athenians; the Spartans; the Persians; various Ionian cities; and personal enemies from sundry other states. Such animosity is unsurprising. Alcibiades was a self-serving psychopath[60] who brought ruin to all who trusted him and did as much as was possible for any one man to destroy even Athens at the height of its powers.

Conclusion

The tumult and the shouting dies
The captains and the kings depart
Still stands thine ancient sacrifice
An humble and a contrite heart
Lord of hosts be with us yet
Lest we forget – lest we forget

Rudyard Kipling, 'Recessional' AD 1897

The world of the fifth century BC may seem remote from our own. Yet the time when the events of this narrative unfolded was exactly the time when the intellectual foundations of the modern world were being laid, and the same people were involved in both. The dynamic, fearless minds that were behind the expedition to Sicily also took a long hard look at the universe that their forefathers had known and ruthlessly reshaped their understanding of it in the hard light of logic. Even today we enjoy the benefits of those insights, and so deeply ingrained is the Athenian perception of the world that today we have difficulty imagining any other. In that sense, we are all Athenians.

The Athenians were inspiring, energetic, unconventional and both physically and intellectually courageous. We should rightly celebrate all these things. But the Athenians of the late fifth century were not good – not good in the eyes of their contemporaries, and certainly not good by the standards of today.

This is a painful admission. There is much that is admirable in the Athenians of the era and we see the fifth century largely through the eyes of Athenian, or pro-Athenian, historians poets and playwrights. But the same intellectual honesty that swept aside the myths and misconceptions of previous eras also forced the Athenians to be clear about what they had done. They had taken allies who had fought shoulder-to-shoulder with them in the cause of freedom and forced them to subservience. Their alliance became an empire that they consciously chose to rule by terror. The small, harmless island population of Melos was massacred and enslaved for no other crime than refusing to surrender its ancient liberty.

The Athenians freely admitted their actions and claimed that imperial powers created their own morality. It was this 'morality' that allowed them to attack the island of Sicily and attempt to subjugate its population. The ethics of conquest were something of a grey area in the Greek world, but even those later irredeemable imperialists, the Romans, at least tried to justify each of their conquests on moral grounds. The Athenians were alone in admitting that what they were doing might be wrong – *but that it did not matter*.

It is this moral vacuum at the heart of Athenian policy that separates it from the 'expeditions' launched by the modern superpowers into far-flung corners of the world. Whatever the outcome in pain and suffering, the protagonists can at least claim they were trying to do good and their enemies were not fellow democracies but odious tyrannies. In the military dimension, too, the modern and ancient expeditions are not comparable. The military adventures in Serbia, Afghanistan and Iraq have been (in the modern military jargon) 'asymmetrical combats' in which one side is massively outgunned. The Athenian expedition was against a state every bit as sophisticated and powerful as itself and is more comparable with the Napoleonic and German invasions of Russia in previous centuries – all the more so because, like the Athenians, the Germans and French had other substantial wars already on their agenda.

So are there lessons for us today in the Athenian expedition to disaster? Thucydides certainly thought so.

> It will be enough for me if my words are found useful to those who want a clear understanding of what happened in the past, and which – since human nature stays the same – will happen again in the future at some time or the other.
>
> Thuc. 1.20

To some extent the tragedy of the Athenian expedition is a morality play written in blood. An empire abandons the values that made it great, and indeed actively turns against those who still hold those values. Yet while the exploitation of the weak and defenceless appears to go unpunished, the blind pride and ambition of the empire eventually over-reaches itself and (with a few deft nudges from fate) collapses into ruin. This is a story that has enjoyed a few re-runs since the fifth century BC, and it is not hard to pick up the plot today.

Among the self-styled elites of today there has been *hubris* on a massive scale, perhaps best exemplified by the words 'too big to fail'. As with the Athenians in Sicily, we see the naked self-interest of a group being given a sophisticated spin to convince the majority that being exploited is actually for the best. Politicians, financiers and large corporations appear to share a separate reality in which ordinary people matter only to the degree they can be gulled or coerced into making good for follies that make the Athenian expedition seem wise by comparison.

Many in today's world have been carelessly damaged by the cynical use of power to satiate greed. Like the Athenians, the perpetrators have paid little attention to Nemesis. The question, perhaps, is whether Nemesis is paying attention to them.

FINIS

Notes

1. Thuc. 3.40. An interesting parallel is this quote from 2002 (just before the invasion of Iraq) and since attributed to George Bush Jnr's aide Karl Rove: 'We're an empire now, and when we act, we create our own reality.' Ron Suskind, *New York Times Magazine*, October 17, 2004.
2. Herod, 5.105.
3. Sparta was celebrating the Karneia, their harvest festival, at the time, and the Spartans took their religion – and almost everything else – very seriously.
4. And the leader was later executed. Cf. Sir William Smith and Charles Anthon, *A New Classical Dictionary of Greek and Roman Biography and Mythology*, Vol. 3, p. 615.
5. Apart from women, criminals, lunatics and slaves, obviously.
6. Plutarch, *Life of Pericles* 4.
7. Thuc. 2.65.
8. Though the extent to which the valley of the Evrotas River provided natural defences is often overlooked.
9. About 60 miles or two-to three-day march.
10. Brasidas at Amphipolis, 422 BC, quoted in Thuc. 5.9.
11. Thuc. 4.85.
12. Plutarch, *Life of Alcibiades* 6.
13. Xenophon's *Hellenica* 2.2 remarks that the Athenians later dreaded that the fate they had inflicted on communities such as Scione would be visited on themselves.
14. The arguments are summarized in Michael G. Seaman's 'The Athenian Expedition to Melos in 416 BC': *Historia: Zeitschrift für Alte Geschichte*, Vol. 46, No. 4 (4th Qtr, 1997), pp. 385–418.
15. Annoyingly, apart from this literary *tour de force*, we have no reports on Athenian deliberations beforehand. For example, the matter must have been hotly debated in the Assembly, but so dominant is the Thucydidian approach that no other ancient authors touch this aspect.
16. 'Alcibiades and Melos: Thucydides 5.84–116', Michael Vicker, *Historia: Zeitschrift für Alte Geschichte*, Vol. 48, No. 3 (3rd Qtr, 1999), pp. 265–81.
17. Plutarch, *Life of Alcibiades* 15.4.
18. Plato Phaedo 109b. For a full discussion on the Greek colonization of the island see Gomme, Andrews and Dover's *Historical commentary on Thucydides* (1945–1981).
19. Thuc. 6.31ff.
20. Ibid. 4.65.3.
21. Diod. 12.82.
22. Diod. 13.2.6.

23. Plutarch, *Life of Nicias* 6.
24. Thuc. 8.73.
25. Ibid. 6.12.
26. Ibid. 6.19.
27. Euelpides in Aristophanes' *Birds* 462.
28. Thuc. 6.31.
29. Plutarch, *Life of Alcibiades* 16.
30. Thuc. 6.30ff.
31. *Inscriptiones Graecae* i 2, 327, 332.
32. Andocides, *On the Mysteries* (the Perseus/Tufts website).
33. There is a lively debate as to how accurate a picture Thucydides has painted of the support for the Athenians in Sicily, and how much was given in terms of men and money. The current trend is to claim that for narrative reasons Thucydides has made the Sicilians less welcoming than was the reality.
34. Plutarch, *Life of Alcibiades* 22.
35. The treatment by Thucydides occasionally does not mesh with the actual geography of the site, causing considerable academic debate over exactly how deployments were arranged. As ever, this battle description is based on my own reading of events.
36. Aeschylus, *Persae* 392–4.
37. Cf. V.D. Hanson (ed.), *Hoplites: The Greek Battle Experience* (Routledge, 1991).
38. Only much later when Syracuse had won a decisive advantage did Camerina declare against Athens in a blatant show of *Realpolitik*.
39. Plutarch, *Life of Alcibiades* 23
40. Aelian V.H. 12.42. It is uncertain whether the Athenians had repaired the bridge by now, but it was still the easiest crossing point.
41. Plutarch, *Life of Nicias* 18.
42. Spartan soldiers famously wore a red battle cloak, and their hair long. Hence the famous scene of the Spartans combing their long tresses before the battle of Thermopylae.
43. Philistus and Timaeus in particular. Plutarch, Life of Nicias 19.
44. J. Morrison, J. Coates and N. Rankov, *The Athenian Trireme: The History and Reconstruction of an Ancient Greek Warship* (Cambridge University Press, 2000).
45. Two other generals were added to the panel: Euthydemos and Menandros. Both were nonentities whom we barely hear of again one Demosthenes arrived.
46. Thuc. 7.28.
47. Just before impact it was a good idea to turn the ramming ship somewhat in the direction the ramee was travelling, since otherwise the forward movement of the ship being rammed might tear off the ram.
48. Morrison, Coates and Rankov, *The Athenian Trireme* (1986 ed.), appendix 1.
49. Thuc. 7.24. It is uncertain where Thucydides got these figures from. Cf. V. D. Hanson, 'Thucydides and the Desertion of Attic Slaves in the Decelean War', *Classical Antiquity* October 1992.
50. More precisely, the Athenians substituted the tribute with an import/export tax of five percent. This was almost certainly to raise further revenue (though this has been disputed). At this time the Athenians had to send home a group of Thracian volunteers whose help they could not afford. This may have turned their minds to the need for more revenue.

51. An inscription has been discovered (IG I 371 l.11), which is apparently a record of payments to Demosthenes for the costs of this force.

52. Diodorus Siculus, 13.10 (note that in this and on matters of chronology Siculus disagrees on occasion with Thucydides, whose account is generally to be preferred where a reconciliation is not possible).

53. Cf. G. Wylie, 'Demosthenes the General: A Protagonist in a Greek Tragedy?' *Greece and Rome* 60, April 1993.

54. Rather as Hindenberg did in his much larger attack of 1918.

55. Plutarch, *Life of Pericles* 35.

56. The synodic lunar month of twenty-nine days, which calculates the movement of the moon on the ecliptic plane, was not used at this time. Had it been, eclipses would have been predictable.

57. In fact, as events were to prove, Athens had more in reserve than this, but Nicias's basic point was valid. Athens could not afford to lose the men and ships of the expedition.

58. Memorably recorded in Xenophon's *Anabasis*, generally known today as 'The March of the Ten Thousand'.

59. The modern village of Floridia. Plutarch, *Life of Nicias* 27.

60. So described by Dr A. Slater in *Predators*, published in 2004, p. 128.

Select Bibliography

Awdry, H. 'A Note on the Walls on Epipolae', *The Journal of Hellenic Studies*, Vol. 29, 1909, pp. 70–78.

Bloedow, E.F. 'The Speeches of Hermocrates and Athenagoras at Syracuse in 415 BC.: Difficulties in Syracuse and in Thucydides', *Historia: Zeitschrift für Alte Geschichte* Bd. 45, H. 2, 2nd Qtr, 1996, pp. 141–58.

Campbell, D. *Ancient Siege Warfare: Persians, Greeks, Carthaginians and Romans 546–146 BC* (Osprey Publishing, 2005).

Dover, K.J. *Thucydides* (Clarendon Press, 1973).

Drögemüller, H. *Syrakus: zur Topographie und Geschichte einer griechischen Stadt.* Gymnasium, Beiheft 6, Heidelberg; Paper, DM.28, 1969, p. 165, 30 plates, 23 maps.

Dummett, J. *Syracuse, City of Legends: A Glory of Sicily* (I.B. Tauris, 2010).

Fields, N. *Syracuse 415–413 BC: Destruction of the Athenian Imperial Fleet* (Osprey Publishing, 2008).

Gomme, A.W., Andrewes, A. and Dover, K.J., *A Historical Commentary on Thucydides* (Oxford University Press USA, 1945–1981).

Hanson, V.D. (ed.), *Hoplites: The Greek Battle Experience* (Routledge, 1991).

Hanson, V.D. 'Thucydides and the Desertion of Attic Slaves in the Decelean War', *Classical Antiquity*, October 1992.

Hanson, V.D. *A War Like No Other: How the Athenians and Spartans Fought the Peloponnesian War* (Random House, 2006).

Holladay, A.J. 'Further Thoughts on Trireme Tactics', *Greece & Rome* Second Series, Vol. 35, No. 2, October 1988, pp. 149–51.

Hornblower, S. *A Commentary on Thucydides: Volume I: Books I–III* (Oxford University Press USA, 1997).

Kallet, L. *Money and the Corrosion of Power in Thucydides: The Sicilian Expedition and its Aftermath* (University of California Press, 2002).

Kelly, D.H. 'What Happened to the Athenians Captured in Sicily?' *The Classical Review* New Series, Vol. 20, No. 2, June 1970, pp. 127–31.

Kelly, T., 'Thucydides and Spartan Strategy in the Archidamian War', *The American Historical Review* Vol. 87, No. 1, February 1982, pp. 25–54.

McGregor, M.F. 'Kleon, Nikias, and the Trebling of the Tribute', *Transactions and Proceedings of the American Philological Association*, Vol. 66, 1935, pp. 146–64.

Morrison, J., Coates, J. and Rankov, N. *The Athenian Trireme: The History and Reconstruction of an Ancient Greek Warship* (Cambridge University Press, 2000).

Robinson, E. 'Democracy in Syracuse, 466–412 B.C.', *Harvard Studies in Classical Philology*, Vol. 100, 2000, pp. 189–205.

Seaman, M.G. 'The Athenian Expedition to Melos in 416 B.C.', *Historia: Zeitschrift für Alte Geschichte*, Vol. 46, No. 4, 4th Qtr, 1997, pp. 385–418.

Strassler, R., Crawley, R. and Hanson, V.D., *The Landmark Thucydides: A Comprehensive Guide to the Peloponnesian War by Thucydides* (Free Press, 1998).

Trevett, J.C. 'Nikias and Syracuse', *Zeitschrift für Papyrologie und Epigraphik* Bd. 106, 1995, pp. 246–8.

Vicker, M. 'Alcibiades and Melos: Thucydides 5.84–116', *Historia: Zeitschrift für Alte Geschichte*, Vol. 48, No. 3, 3rd Qtr, 1999, pp. 265–81.

Wallinga, H.T., 'The Trireme and History', *Mnemosyne* Fourth Series, Vol. 43, Fasc. 1/2, 1990, pp. 132–49.

Wylie, G. 'Demosthenes the General – A Protagonist in a Greek Tragedy?', *Greece and Rome*, Vol. 40, April 1993, pp. 20–30.

Index